GEMS
FOR THE TAKING

GEMS
FOR THE TAKING

❧ ❧ ❧

Mine Your Own Treasure

MARY L. T. BROWN

The Macmillan Company, *New York, New York*

Collier-Macmillan Ltd., London

The Macmillan Company
866 Third Avenue, New York, N.Y. 10022
Collier-Macmillan Canada Ltd., Toronto, Ontario
Library of Congress Catalog Card Number: 70–130945

Second Printing 1971

PRINTED IN THE UNITED STATES OF AMERICA

ACKNOWLEDGMENTS

Special thanks to George Downing and his gem-studded family who introduced me to the world of gemstones; to Robert Crowningshield, Director of the Gemological Institute of America, in New York, who so kindly edited this book for errors about the mineral kingdom; to Dr. Ernest H. Rutland of the Geological Survey, London, England, for his time and information; and to all the people who have laced the centuries with gem lore.

To my Mother—
the lady of the
topaz eyes!

CONTENTS

1

⟁

Ruby Fever!

Life can be a dazzling adventure, but we are so accustomed to thinking that the best things in the cosmos start at a price of twenty thousand dollars most of us never explore the treasures, the literal treasures, that are all around us.

A handful of gems, especially rubies, is something we tend to link with a maharajah or oriental legend. I did too, until a friend invited me to join him and his family on a ruby safari that took me from the air-polluted charms of New York to the cool mountains of North Carolina. An absolute amateur, I mined for only five days and unearthed eight exquisite rubies and twenty-one extraordinary sapphires, some of which have been called "collectors' delights."

The smallest ruby I found was the first one I mined. It was 1.72 carats and worth about $175. Not a bad beginning when you consider that the investment up to that point had been less than twenty cents for the pail of soil in which I found my crimson gemstone. Added to this was a two-dollar entrance fee covering the cost of the entire day on which I found several other stones, mostly unusual sapphires.

During the week I was there—we mined from Monday to Friday—I found almost a mayonnaise jar full of smaller rubies and sapphires, but they did not have either the size or the perfection of the twenty-nine stones that the gemologist in Highlands cut and polished to dazzling beauty.

Ruby Fever is a disease that one contracts by word of mouth. It affects almost everyone in the same way. Generally a good friend—because only such a friend will confide the location of his treasure trove—tells you that he, his family, and perhaps their water spaniel have been ruby mining and wouldn't you like to join them some time. You, of course, are all dropped mouth and flip-flap ears.

"Yes," you say sweetly, "what's the catch?" and "Aren't you a little old for glue sniffing?"

"No catch," he says. But you don't believe him—quite.

"Start at the beginning," you say, suddenly a stickler for the definite.

"Well," he drawls, "there's a little place in North Carolina where we've been mining for some years." Then he whips out a piece of bulky white cotton around which is a rubber band. Casually, with just that bit of nonchalance that drops your mouth another two inches, he displays a bracelet he just had set for his wife or his daughter. It is studded with some of the most beautiful pale sapphires you have ever seen, and the clasp is a ruby as big as a bean.

"You mined those?" you ask, when your mouth is able to move up and down again.

"The children got most of them," he says offhandedly, plunging you instantaneously into that abyss known as RUBY FEVER.

"How can I get away at this time of the year?" you wail to no one in particular as you mentally check railroad timetables, your work schedule, and the possibility of finding a mate to the Black Prince's Ruby. Golconda is a dim vision, North Carolina is instant paradise, and the train fare, you find, is less than the price of a Jack McConnell hat.

Ruby mining is not an arduous pastime. I was one of the few miners who made it a day's work. My mining companions tended to do it more as a lark than the deadly serious business it became for me. After all, I had only five days, and at times I acted like the poor soul who has only twelve minutes for lunch. My friends, of course, had been mining for years; and there are just so many rubies and sapphires you can wear to any one outing.

Everyone teased me about the tireless, eyeball-to-stones confrontations I made as I hosed down the basket of soil to separate the gleam and values of the real gems from the gravel and stones that needed to be discarded. The greatest terror of surface mining is the fear that you have thrown away a precious gem because you did not recognize it.

But ruby mining is more than just getting to the mine and extracting its treasures. The anticipation, the hunt, the discovery, the delights of the appraisal by experts afterward are all bound up in the delicious affliction of Ruby Fever. If you would like to know exactly how it is done, hereby hangs a true tale.

2

Ruby Country

The railroad coach was almost steaming with heat as we
neared Toccoa, a little town in north Georgia. I squirreled
around in the prickly mohair seat until I felt more like a
pinwheel than a person. I had transferred to the smaller,
stifling car from my comfortable, air-conditioned Pullman
only an hour before. My face gleamed like a shined dime, and
the rest of me was baked soggy by the temperature that
seemed to be 130 degrees inside the train.

If this is what it takes to get to Toccoa, I promised myself,
this is my first and last trip. And I tried to lose myself in some
mental calisthenics. One of the things I remember doing was
an exploration of Dimnet's theory of the natural creativity of
children. *Any child,* I told myself, *would have enough sense
not to come on the fool's errand this promises to be, and
certainly not by rail.* My great character flaw is that I am a
train addict and will leap aboard anything that is moving out
of a railroad terminal.

A lady across the aisle, quite awesome because she reminded me of a piece of polychromatic sculpture, kindly
offered me a fan. It was a commercial one, advertising Coca-
Cola on cubes of ice. Just looking at it helped, and I flung it
back and forth in front of my face until the conductor came
by to say we were coming into Toccoa station. I might say
there are easier ways of getting to the mining area than the
covered wagon routes I pursue, but I am a born traveler who
must see every river and scratch bark from every tree.

(Toccoa, Georgia, is about fifty miles from Highlands,

North Carolina, where we stayed, and sixty-five miles from Franklin, where we mined. One can go by air to Asheville, North Carolina, or to Greenville, South Carolina. Greenville seems to have a better flying schedule. Then, take a bus or car, if possible, to Franklin, North Carolina. I understand an airport has been under construction in the heart area of the mines.)

My friends, who were all from one family, were swarming over the station platform as I staggered out into slightly drier heat. Their welcome was warmer than the climate but considerably more agreeable. We all piled into an old station wagon that was part of a colorful caravan of cars. Soon it sounded like a birdhouse, with everyone chirping and giving advice on a different facet of mining. Dogs, children, and grown-ups were making music that would force the chorus angelorum to cringe.

We outrode the heat quickly as we got near the mountains. Soon we had left Georgia and were heading up the more than four thousand feet to Highlands, where my friends had rented a replica of an old English manor house. The structure was big, smoky, sprawling—and very inviting. It seemed to have a hundred doors and windows and all of them appeared to be in motion as soon as the car stopped.

A very small boy, the only member of the family who had not gone to the station, marched up to me with determined, short steps and put what looked like a large lavender and white crystal into my hand.

"Teddy, where did you get that?" asked the head of the house, relieving me of the pastel treasure.

"Upstairs," said Teddy over his shoulder, disappearing into the house as fast as he had emerged.

My host, who had led me to a chair on the beautiful stone porch that overlooked the valley, put the lavender crystal on the table in front of us.

"Amethyst," he said laconically. "One of our boys found it on the trail beyond the house."

It was almost too much. I was ready to mine for possible

rubies, but I wasn't prepared to walk on amethysts. The whole thing began to seem like an outrageous fairy tale, and I was a bit shaky as I followed my hostess through the old house to my room. A warm bath would make everything seem real again.

3

Preparing for the Mines

I slept that first night like a child in the arms of the fairies. When I awoke, the sun was sending crazy streamers into my room even as I shivered under the two blankets demanded by the mountain cool. I bathed, dressed in my idea of a chic mining costume, and went down to breakfast.

The entire family, including dogs and turtles, was assembled in the big dining room when my *beaucoup couture* burst upon them. I was wearing white slacks and a black and white striped sweater and had covered my scrambled little head with a snow-colored chiffon scarf. I was dazzling—for about four seconds. With the efficiency and dispatch for which this family was to become famous—or infamous, depending on whom they were practicing their fiery art—they noted, rated, and discounted my white à la mode. Wordlessly, but quickly, I was wrapped from shoulders to ankles in a plastic dry cleaner's bag. Then a small voice said it for all of them. . . . "She looks like a box of candy, Dad."

I don't know if you have ever tried to eat hominy grits or even a bacon sandwich from the warm vacuum of a dry cleaner's transparency, but my cool friends saw nothing unusual in the puffs of cellophane that billowed and fell over the table as I bit and swallowed. Before the end of the week I was to become notorious for the weird, protective clothing patterns I would carry to the mines. I think it is the memory of those costumes that keeps me from growling at the flower children. However, with breakfast over, it was rubies not Balenciagas that were on my mind.

Everyone participated in making the picnic lunch, as min-ing is generally an all-day affair. I was always transfixed by the incredibly thin layer of butter that Margaret, the maid, spread over the bread. Doradelle, a delightful relative of my host, and a lady to whom the joys of the table—as to all of us—meant somewhat as much as mining, complained bitterly each day about the transparent promise of butter and each morning Margaret made it an artistic fetish to see how lightly she could spread it *that* day.

Doradelle and I contributed little more than advice and putting back mayonnaise jar covers. But as we stood waiting for the goodies to be slipped into their waxed bags, Doradelle told tales of her other mining adventures and dropped little tidbits about the organ in *her* kitchen. Somehow, her stories made every kitchen in the world that didn't have an organ seem unequipped. When the organ stories ran down she would plunge into reminiscences of the fascinating exploits of her unique husband, Bricks. They not only shared a house that had an organ in the kitchen but that had an oriental rug and a fireplace as well. And in the living room of their cedar-shingled house, standing like Miss Liberty herself among priceless antiques, was their beloved lapidary machine for cutting and polishing gems. It was exactly the kind of house you would expect of a man who had built his own jeep.

Highlands, where we were staying, is over 4,200 feet above sea level at its lowest elevation. It is the highest town of its population east of the Rockies. Our lovely old house was 150 feet from the top of Satullah Mountain, fanned night and day by crisp breezes.

Because everyone had become infected or reinfected with my exotic disease, Ruby Fever, we fairly flew down the moun-tain roads and onto the route to Franklin about nineteen miles away. The Cowee Valley ruby mines are about ten miles beyond that, and there is no absence of signs to point the way.

My curiosity about the specifics of how the gem material

found its way to that part of the world was satisfied by my host, George Downing, who with his delightful family has mined in dozens of places in North America, and whose gem collection is breathtaking.

He told me the large variety of gem material in North Carolina is attributable to the fact that the Appalachian Mountains are known to be among the oldest mountains in the world. There is geological proof that their elevation once exceeded the height of any mountains extant in the world today. This, of course, is proven by the build-up of sediment in the Continental Shelf both in the Gulf of Mexico and the Atlantic Ocean. And as these mountains have worn down over the years the gem materials have come to light.

The Cowee Valley is in Macon County. Besides rubies and sapphires (the corundums) Macon County also produces garnets, rhodolite garnets (a rare pale, rosy garnet), emerald or aquamarine (beryl), and amethyst (quartz).

According to the North Carolina Department of Conservation and Development,

> Macon County has several corundum [ruby and sapphire] deposits which were originally worked primarily for abrasives and secondarily for gem stones. With the replacement of artificial abrasives after the turn of the century, the mining of these deposits ceased.
>
> The Cowee Creek rubies occur in association with rhodolite garnet, sillimanite, staurolite, iolite, monazite, gold [see, you mustn't skip a word] pyrite, chalcopyrite, pyrrotite, shalerite, sperrylite, ilmenite, rutile, bronzite, hornblende, zircon and kyanite in the stream deposits of the Caler Fork of Cowee Creek. This deposit is located 1.9 miles east of West Mills and six miles north of Franklin. Some of the rubies are of the valued pigeon-blood color and are said to equal in color and brilliancy the Burma rubies.

(This is true because one of the most knowledgeable men in the Gemological Institute saw my North Carolina rubies

and without knowing their origin said, "ah, someone has been to Burma." The extent of this compliment can only be realized when you know that the Burma rubies are considered the best in the world. There is little doubt about it, the rubies found in limestone in Cowee Creek are as lovely as rubies found anywhere.)

The North Carolina Department of Conservation and Development continues:

> Corundum Hill, located 1.5 miles east of the village of Cullassaja, produced a large quantity of abrasive corundum as well as ruby [what was formerly called oriental emerald and oriental amethyst, and blue and yellow sapphire].
>
> The Raby Mine, near Burningtown Creek, 1.2 miles southwest of Burningtown, contains well-crystallized pink and purple corundum. The Mincey Mine, located about 0.7 of a mile east of Ellijay and seven miles southeast of Franklin, has produced some bronze corundum, which, when properly polished, shows asterism.
>
> Corundum, in association with rutile, asbestos and vermiculite is reported in the vicinity of Bernette Lake in the Scaly community, 5.5 miles southwest of Highlands.

One must constantly check out mine locations as mines frequently open and close to the public and change their rules and patterns from season to season. Also, always get permission to mine if you are on private property. You just might find a gemstone YOU CAN'T KEEP.

Well, we were off. We were in Macon County, and we were racing past Franklin. The area was alive with gemstones and our adventurous spirit, especially mine, was at fever level.

"Let's try Ruth Holbrook's place first," suggested our gem-learned leader, who had already phoned her to say there would be seven of us.

4

The First Day

As we drove up to the Holbrook Mine my loose mouth fell open again. In front of us was a beautiful old house, mallow-colored, with four inviting picnic tables set out under fruit and elm trees. Old-fashioned green and white awnings blew like friendly flags from every window.

As we trooped out of the long car, young Teddy began gesturing excitedly in the direction of a large hole in what appeared to be the side of a grassless lawn. "There it is. There it is. There it is." He gurgled on the last word, too overcome with excitement to expel another syllable.

"There's what?" I wanted to know.

"The mine," chorused six voices.

It was indeed a day of surprises. Where were the deep caverns? Where were the miners with lights atop their caps? *There was* a hole the size of a wagon, and everyone agreed it was THE MINE. Then the charm and the natural delight of the whole thing reached me. What a marvelous idea—growing rubies . . . in one's own back yard. I was about to learn "surface mining" firsthand.

"Disappointed?" asked a deep, confident voice at my side, and I turned to greet the owner. Tall and tanned leathery by the valley sun, Ruth Holbrook has to be the warmest note that has ever been played in the Southern hospitality symphony. She pumped my hand up and down like a butter churn, and it all added up to an overwhelming friendliness. Later I learned she had been a trained nurse, and of inestimable help to Dr. Angel, who, with his brother, helped build the hospital in Franklin.

Without making me feel as though I had three feet that all pointed in the wrong direction, she guided me to one of what seemed to be about fifteen large filing trays with sieve bottoms. They were set on table frames that were waist high. A water hose was connected to each tray.

"Where are the picks and shovels?" I was quick with questions.

"Oh," I was informed, "Willard will do the digging." I began to wonder what my part in all this would be. Was the actual mining done by telephone?

"Diggin' is very tirin'," Ruth Holbrook explained. "Your arms will be twitchin' like a hungry coyote with an eye on a rabbit just from hosin' down the stones."

Willard, another jewel in the South's hospitality crown, appeared with a wheelbarrow heaped high with soil. He filled six water pails with the soil, which was mixed with gravel, and placed them near me. Then he took the first one and emptied one-half of it into my sieve-bottom tray.

Everyone was watching me. . . .

"I'm the biggest amateur around here," I blubbered. . . . "HELP!"

I was a little shocked that there were no stools. Since I was prepared to spend the day there I was a little put off by the fact that I would be standing . . . until I began to mine. Then everything went out of my head except the fascinating game of "ruby, ruby, who has the . . . sapphire, maybe?"

Both rubies and sapphires are corundum, a major aluminum mineral, *ergo*, sapphires are likely to be found in the same "home"—the same mineral situation—as rubies.

It is interesting to note that the word *corundum* is associated with the French word *corindon*, which comes from the old Tamilian word *kurundam*. In Sanskrit corundum is called the *kuruvinda* ruby. These gemstones originally made their way to Europe from India. The hexagonal form of crystal is typical of the ruby and sapphire or corundum, so look for crystal formations that are six-sided.

Pure corundum is colorless, as most gem materials are when they are chemically pure. It is the different metallic oxides that add color. The ruby is colored red by minute amounts of chromium (chromic oxide) and the sapphire is colored blue by faint traces of iron and titanium. The other shades such as pink, yellow, green, purple, and orange hues of sapphire are colored by other metallic oxides.

Stones like the sapphire, ruby and emerald (the mineral, beryl), which depend on *impurities* for their color are called allochromatic. Stones that have lively colors even when pure are known as idiochromatic.

Green corundum has sometimes been called oriental emerald; yellow corundum is known as oriental topaz; and purple corundum is called oriental amethyst.

Perfectly colorless stones are quite uncommon as one is likely to find at least a slight bluish tint in corundum. The "white sapphire" can never be mistaken for the diamond because no amount of faceting could lend diamond "fire" to the albino corundum. Unlike the green garnet or the white zircon, which have some of the fire of the diamond, the colorless corundum or white sapphire is quite dull, and is in no demand since it does not have the one thing colorless stones must have to be prized gemstones—*brilliancy*.

The word *sapphire* is probably of Semitic origin, but it has as many alleged derivations as the books you will read on it. There is the Syriac *saphilah*, a name which indicates the stone in the Syrian tongue, but there is also the Hebrew *sappir*, and the Greek *sappheiros*. I have also known it to be associated with the island Sapphirine in the Arabian Sea. Sapphire is a word that somehow has beauty and music in any language.

Ruby comes from the Latin *rubeus*, red. This is the only corundum not called sapphire. In spite of some shades of corundum being called the oriental version of emerald, topaz, and amethyst, generally, the name sapphire is rightly applied to any corundum *but red.* I might say here that the so-called oriental amethyst seems to unite the ruby-red and sapphire-blue to produce an incredible violet hue. This is a very scarce stone indeed. Henry Thomas Hope, after whom the Hope Diamond was named, had an oriental amethyst of great beauty in his famous gem collection.

The sapphire is a stone that seems to have inherited a legend of gender. The light sapphires were considered female and the darker variety were thought to be male by some of the ancients. This will give you some idea of the way in which the people of yesterday thought of gems as living things. Minerals, of course, are naturally occurring *inorganic* chemical elements or compounds.

More common than rubies, sapphires are, therefore, less valuable. The cornflower-blue shade of sapphire is the most desirable hue. Artificial light adds great brightness to that particular shade of gem. Long ago it was the royal-blue shade of sapphire that was lauded and in great demand. Its dark beauty is somewhat lost in the fashions of today.

The ruby varies in shades of red—I have found several hues in just one mining area in North Carolina—but the pigeon's blood-red, the red that veers toward purple, is the greatly sought-after shade of the gem. And that is what we considered *our* ultimate prize.

It somehow reduces the romance of the entire project to hear it, but ruby and sapphire have been called crystallized clay. Chemically the ruby and sapphire are pure alumina. While they are identical chemically, they are quite different in appearance (you remember those minute bits of metallic oxides: chromium, iron, titanium). Both stones are grouped in Mohs' Scale of Hardness as 9. (There may be a small, difficult-to-prove difference in their hardness that will be mentioned later.) The only gemstone with greater hardness than the ruby and the sapphire is the diamond. This concentration on hardness is not a flimsy or arbitrary thing. To be a gemstone of truly precious proportions there must be not only beauty and purity, but the hardness that ensures durability. Gems come on the scene to last a long, long time—through the centuries—and every age that has known their beauty has been inspired and enriched by them.

Here is Mohs' Scale as it goes from the softest to the hardest mineral. This table is relative, not actual, and does not indicate the same distance between the hardness of various minerals. Number 10, the diamond, can scratch all of them and each one from 10 to 2 can scratch the mineral (number) before it, as the lower number is softer.

1. Talc

2. Gypsum

3. Calcite

4. Fluorite

5. Apatite

6. Orthoclase

7. Quartz

8. Topaz

9. Corundum

10. Diamond

The hardest of any two substances will scratch the softer. Although ruby and sapphire (corundum) are listed as 9 they are *considerably* softer than the diamond—infinitely more than their numerical distance would indicate. And the sapphire, although corundum like the ruby, is considered slightly harder than its red sister by some experts and is the precious stone next to the diamond in hardness. In the same manner, aquamarine, the semiprecious variety of beryl, is considered by some to be slightly harder than the precious emerald, which might not quite measure up to the hardness of its sturdier partner. Robert Crowningshield of the Gemological Institute of America says there is no actual test that can prove these slight differences in hardness of the same mineral that many jewelers believe in. He thinks the belief in the difference is due to the abundance of the less costly variety of corundum and beryl, as they produce more specimens that endure.

As you begin to mine here in North America be grateful that you can find and mine sapphires yourself that are so close to home. There were days when finding a good group of sapphires meant going to Siam and squeezing the hand of a Siamese miner for days on end in code signals until the proper bargain was reached. By the time the sapphires were ready to be delivered, the poor gem merchant was probably barely able to lift his fingers to receive them.

AND NOW . . . BACK TO THE RUBY MINES!

Washing ruby gravel, or what you hope will be ruby- or sapphire-bearing gravel, is easy. You just take the hose in one hand as you would to sprinkle your lawn, while you agitate the soil and stones with your other hand. Soon the soil disappears through the sieve openings and only stones are left, and that is when panic sets in. How *will* you tell a ruby? Actually, the real problem is how do you tell a sapphire, as they are almost always as protectively colored as they are abundant when they come from the mine pits. The rubies rather jump out at you because they look much like their ultimate color self, even in their rawest form.

I washed down the first tray of gravel until every stone looked the color of milk. Everyone suggested I throw away the lot and empty the rest of the pail of soil to see what the other half would bring. In spite of all the joshing I really had gem jitters, and would not release the well-watered gravel until everyone nearby had inspected the stones and assured me there was not a single gem hiding among them.

For reasons known only to a higher power I was a quick

study, and soon I was able to identify tiny sapphires even
Willard or the others missed. Of course, I was teased beyond
belief for the way I mined. I leaned so low and peered so
intently into the tray that I more than once received an eyeful
of water from my own hose as well as a close look at the
stones.

I was most proud of the way the silvery-brown and purple
hue of the sapphires began to leap out and identify themselves. They had an instant glaze under the water that looked
like the sheen of mica. Their luster or surface gloss identified
them each time.

By lunch time, a call I answered reluctantly in spite of the
sylvan setting of our picnic table, I had three rather good-
sized sapphires and two not-so-large rubies (or so I thought).
I was like a bumblebee during lunch and my mining companions excused me early and tolerantly so I could get back to my
tray. In seconds I was sifting the gravel mixture with the
confidence and second wind of a professional miner. The day
ended with three more sapphires in the little plastic pill bottle
that each of us carried to hold our daily finds.

5

❧

The Treasure's Worth

I had mined without one spadeful of digging, and I was as utterly exhausted as someone who had dug a dozen ditches that day. However, I was determined, before I left the mines after my so-called "holiday," to go down into the garden hole to "mine" at least once and try to dig out a few baubles myself. A senseless pastime, I can tell anyone. You cannot recognize the gemstones until you hose them down anyway unless they are as big as grapes, and the time and energy wasted in digging can be incalculable.

One of the more piercing joys of one's first day of mining is the visit to the gemologist to have the stones appraised. We stopped at Archie Jellen's shop in Highlands on the way home, and I was so tired after we got out of the car I could hardly climb the uncommonly high curb in front of his shop.

Archie Jellen and his wife, Hazel, are not only gem authorities but artists in creating settings for the stones that are found. He was incredibly kind and quickly ran the stones through his light to see which were pure enough to polish. *Purity is the rarest quality of a ruby*, and our ruby finds were our great concern. A moment after Mr. Jellen began to examine the stones he was nodding approvingly. I felt like the Empress of Persia. "You have some good ones here . . . this ruby especially," he said. Later, when it had been polished, he was to tell me that this, my first mined ruby, was 1.72 carats and worth about $175. I left the stones with him for cutting and polishing and with feet that barely touched the ground accepted his invitation to look in his huge vault at some of the gems that had been set in exquisite mountings and also to view some of the staggeringly beautiful jewels in his multiple display cases.

Hazel Jellen does most of the designing, creating breathtaking frames that add fresh dimensions to the natural beauty of the gems. A talented Belgian does the gold work after Mrs. Jellen sketches out the design.

The Jellen shop is a conglomerate of so many things the treasures are almost lost there. Stuffed animals are all over the shop, and in some instances costume jewelry sits side by side with a positive treasure trove. Rough stones of every kind, shape, and color make you blink and wonder where to look first . . . and then next.

Besides an emerald stamp box we will discuss later, Archie Jellen has one treasure he is very unlikely to sell. One day he bought a collection of arrowheads, and a pigeon's blood-red, perfectly shaped arrowhead ruby was among the lot. It had undoubtedly been used as a ceremonial piece. He has been offered more than six thousand dollars for the Indian rarity, which is about two inches by one and one-half inches. Recently a lady of obvious means offered $165,000 for just such an arrowhead. The Indians were familiar with uncountable numbers of gems, and the rich red of the ruby must have charmed them for more than just its durability. Always enamored of gemstones, the Indians used them as charms, pulverized them into powder for medicine men, used them as amulets, and for ceremonials of one kind or another. Whenever one thinks of the Indian as primitive, he must remember how early the quick eye of the redman sought out the beauty of gemstones and utilized them as a daily delight.

I wandered around the treasures in the Jellen shop like a child on a Sunday picnic—gleeful. Each gem I saw reminded me that all of them had been found in North America and here indeed was a continent where the gems are plentiful and "for the taking."

Some days in your life taste sweeter than others. That first day of a new adventure, surface mining, filtered into an evening of tired delight . . . and I went to sleep with visions of gems, large and small, sifting through my fingers like rice.

6

❧

More Luck at the Mines . . . A Day of Famine

On the second day of mining, I was just as eager as ever but not quite as fresh. We started a little later that morning for the mines, as all of us needed the extra rest. When we arrived at Ruth Holbrook's place I was crushed to find all the places were taken. Since there was only room for fifteen at the small mine, I felt fortunes were being lost with each minute we studied the backs of the other miners. You can imagine my relief when the owner told us the visitors were some old friends and would be there only until they finished the single pail of soil she had given each one.

The extra hour gave me a chance to go over to the big garden hole and examine it more closely. Many people insisted on doing their own digging as the two-dollar entrance fee entitled them to dig all day. Either people did not know or did not care to take advantage of the generous six-pails-for-a-dollar offer of the owner . . . who gave the money to the boy who dug the soil. For that reason their mining was comparatively slow and our finds were many times more abundant.

Once down in the mine itself, which was like a trench and just waist high at that time, every bit of soil looked like every other bit of soil or "gem gravel" as it is more properly called. To spot a ruby or a sapphire there you would need eyesight that was gem-magnetic. By the time the visitors had restored our mining trays to us I had lost my adventurous spirit about "digging" and was ready to attack the soil in my box with enthusiasm and the supreme confidence of a seasoned miner.

It just never occurred to me that I would not find treasure every time I bent my head.

The day was a gala one. The rubies and sapphires trickled into my little pill bottle in goodly numbers. Of course all of them would not be flawless and fit for polishing into jewelry, but more than half of them were later found to be first-class, precious gems.

As on the previous day we left the stones at Archie Jellen's place and departed for the cool of our homey stone citadel, high on the mountain. Once you begin to mine you also begin to take an interest in everything else that grows out of the earth around you. A short walk along the beautiful, natural paths that ran in all directions from the house unearthed exquisite stones and breathtaking flora. These in themselves, together with the indescribable mountain sunsets, made the trip to North Carolina a dazzling experience. One wonders why beautiful spots like this are not saluted more often. One panoramic wonder after the other leaped at you in those lovely Blue Ridge Mountains. Every stray glance encountered landscapes worthy of an artist's brush. All I could think was *All this beauty created for the enjoyment of man and he sits in some smoky city somewhere wrinkling his brow over his wife's charge accounts or some other man-made monster.*

On the third day there was much buzzing in the pantry where preparing the picnic lunch had become a group festival. The helpers, as usual, were more given to opinion than motion. As always, I stood in mute admiration as Margaret filmed the bread with her teasing veil of butter while Doradelle glowered. The buzzing became louder and nearer and it had to do with going to a different mine. This day we would go to Gibson's. It was larger than the Holbrook Mine and they had a record of some good "finds" there. Eager to increase my knowledge of surface mining, I was delighted to try a different type of it. I said "tally-ho" or whatever one says to get the mining show on the road with a confirming vote, and once again we were off on a day's mining junket.

The Gibson Mine is near Ruth Holbrook's place, but that is where the similarity ends. As we drew up, instead of the single car of the owner and a few other vehicles, there was a huge parking lot, and dozens of cars with license plates from many different states were snugly settled. We appeared to have numerical competition, at least, at this spot.

The mining at Gibson's is entirely different from that at the first mine. The sluice box is used and it is a trough type operation. They sat us down on very low seats beside a narrow trough that extended, perhaps, one hundred feet. The seat was too low for my long legs, so that unless I sat like a man, holding the tray in front of me in the running water, the tray leaped out of my hands and the stones went flying in all directions. In any event I must have been one of the more awkward miners in that manner, but I needn't have perfected my technique. The day was a total disaster. Not one member of our party found even a spotted stone, and it was entirely our fault. It seems the bulldozers were preparing to dig out some new soil to unearth fresh gem gravel and *we had arrived a day too early.* That's an important factor. Right after new depths or wider areas have been dug out is the ideal time for finding large numbers of good gemstones. Gibson's is a very lively, gem-bearing mine as some of our other house guests were to prove before I left North Carolina. I have been told Mr. Gibson himself has a ruby that was found in a sapphire. You can't ask any more than a gem within a gem from any mining expedition.

By three o'clock even I, the most enthusiastic member of the party, was ready to call it a day. My spirits were very low indeed, and everyone enjoyed my dejection because I had been the cheery voice of "never say die" since my arrival. Now, it was difficult to convince me the entire gem output of the Cowee Valley had not dried up.

Once again we piled into the old station wagon and headed for home by way of Archie Jellen's. "Let's see what wonders Archie has wrought from yesterday's labors," suggested our wise host, hoping to raise our spirits with evidence of former triumphs. It turned out to be a good idea. When we arrived, and our arrival was always clamorous, Archie Jellen had his "there's good news tonight" smile ready for us. He told us there were some collector's gems among the stones, including some of mine. He said I had a dark green sapphire that was unique and a black sapphire that could be made into a double cabochon. . . . not to forget, either, a ruby or two that were asteriated—and large. One of these was later appraised for approximately two thousand dollars. Well, there is nothing more likely to make a frustrated miner happy in a hurry than finding out a half dozen stones she was a bit unsure of are indeed good gem quality.

My depression lifted instantaneously. The others, who had been living vicariously since my arrival, were so pleased at my luck they began to feel cheery again too. None of us demurred when our host suggested it might be a good evening to dine at the country club, since it was early enough for us to bathe and rest before a gala dinner.

The evening became a blaze of gem fashions as my hostess and Doradelle wore some of their loveliest stones. Doradelle had a ruby on her finger that was the size of any jelly bean I have ever seen. She had found it in North Carolina. Jean Downing, my hostess, wore a bracelet made from milky cabochon sapphires she had personally mined. It was set in exquisite gold links, a song of sapphires in starry pastels. I wore my charm bracelet and . . . hope.

7

❧

Return to Holbrook Mine

Without consultation we had all decided to return to Holbrook's. We were almost superstitious about our luck there. Ruth Holbrook was out to greet us as though she had stayed up all night to perform the ritual. I think she missed the excitement of our enthusiasm. Our spirits, especially mine, were always on parade. Most people who mine seem to be very low key. It is almost as though they were finding the gems illicitly. They talk in low tones, and put head to head to discuss whether what they have just unearthed "is one," or "isn't one."

We had early-morning luck and it made all of us surer than ever that our best days would be at Holbrook's place. When we went off to lunch among the trees there was the great satisfaction of having several successful hours behind us. Also, one never knows the actual quality of the stones he has found, so there was that lovely anticipation of the later appraisal to nibble on.

Each evening as I returned to Highlands I took my rejects (the stones Archie Jellen thought were not quite good enough to polish and cut into more than chips) and put them into a mayonnaise jar and started each new day with my small, plastic pill bottle. That day I had brought along the mayonnaise jar itself, empty, because I so strongly felt I would find all kinds of interesting stones. I began to feel emerald hungry, but none of us found an emerald anywhere that week. However, my mining companions did find emeralds in other parts of the South as I shall describe later.

When we returned from lunch everyone wanted to help me, and someone put my pail of soil and gravel into my tray before I could do so. I had been hosing for a few seconds when the largest red stone I ever hope to see showed through the wet, glossy mixture. My excitement was acute until I saw the mischievous smiles around me. . . . Ruth Holbrook had painted a plum-sized stone to a ruby red color and slipped it into my pail. Since the children there were bursting at the seams at the joke, I had to act it through, but for thirty-odd seconds I *had* thought I had the biggest gem find since the De Long Ruby.

Ruth Holbrook has a habit that many miners, including Doradelle, pursue. She puts stones in her mouth as she finds them. Since her eye is as trained as anyone's you could find, she was frequently able to walk past the wheelbarrow or the mine and separate a gemstone from the soil as she sifted through it without a hose. Today she wanted me to have a healthy jarful of stones so she spat, in mountain style, two fair-sized sapphires into my tray. Willard came by with a stone he thought might be a green sapphire and contributed that. It turned out to be just that, and was most interesting when polished. With so many people making play out of work and with hospitality a byword, it was difficult to think of leaving such an oasis of good cheer and riches, but my days in treasure valley were indeed numbered . . . like five.

8

☙

Mining . . . and Other Fun

Lest it seem that life as a miner on holiday is a hard-eyed battle with soil and soot, I must say we savored every minute of the beautiful scenery and the glorious weather. As we stood at the tables hosing down the stones, the sun nuzzled our backs but the breeze was refreshingly cool and blew our cares into the mountains. It was one of the most healthful, picturesque regions I ever hope to visit.

Leaving the mines on Friday evening was like tearing oneself away from an old friend, and we had, indeed, made friends. Willard was like another arm, and there was never a moment when Ruth Holbrook did not make us feel we were her very special guests. There was, indisputably, a greater treasure at those mines than the rubies and sapphires we found there.

With the week of mining behind us we had been promised a delicious evening at the charming inn at Highlands. You come upon it suddenly, having ridden 4,200 feet above sea level, and it is as though it had been dropped out of the mist. Friday was one of those evenings that seem made for fiesta. Pungent with fragrance, it was as though someone had wrung out the flowers to scent the night. As we drove near, the amber lights of the inn shone through the trees. It seemed to be hanging there like a giant, golden lantern.

We had dressed with great care and all of us felt quite festive as we walked up the steps of the charming old house. The other ladies in the party were quite heavy with gem treasures. I wound my gold watch continually to show I was on the gold standard, at least, and I fingered my Ceylon sapphire ring, which looked increasingly smaller and cloudier alongside those gorgeous one-of-a-kind gems my friends were wearing. Archie Jellen had promised to cut, polish, and mail my stones to me in about a month, because it would take that long to finish the large assortment I had left with him, so I was not wearing any of my gem finds.

One of the unwritten rules of gem miners is that you talk about gems and gem mining whether you are brushing your teeth (no easy feat), dining out, having a Gatorade, or practicing Yoga. So, as usual, the talk turned to our favorite subject.

The people who mined with me were most generous with their information, and my host and his family were always tossing away little gems of knowledge. They jumped from instruction to gem lore so the evenings out were a pure delight. Even I found it possible to contribute a tidbit when the talk lagged, which wasn't often.

For instance, one of the better ways to examine a stone if you wish to know more specifically why the gemologist either rated it high or rejected it for polishing and setting, is to look at it through a magnifying glass near the rim of a lighted lamp shade. Something that looked quite perfect to you in your hand can look mighty speckled and otherwise imperfect using that test. Jean Downing, my hostess, was so keen-eyed and so skilled at recognizing a good gem that she made the lampshade test before she brought her gems to be appraised and she was usually right in her estimate.

It is not easy to know the true identity of gems. It had been rumored that the famous Black Prince's Ruby was not a ruby at all but a "balas ruby" or red spinel. Of course, since that particular "ruby" is part of the royal regalia of England it was some time before anyone definitely shook up the royal household with cries of "spinel, spinel" sounding up and down the corridors of Buckingham Palace. Actually, it is now an accepted fact that the Black Prince's "Ruby" *is* spinel. You might note that even spinel is specifically identified. The ruby-red shade is called "red spinel" and the paler shade of red is (incorrectly) called "balas ruby."

As we lingered over our cool appetizers longer than the hovering waiters might have liked, everyone warmed to the subject.

"Are you aware," said a voice of authority I was in no position to refute, "that a ruby is said to turn green when heated and return to red when it cools." Perhaps, perhaps, but no one is ever going to prove it by the amount of rubies I am ever likely to drop into the fire.

Since the sapphire is my birthstone I was pleased to discover sapphires are the stones associated with intelligence. According to the ancients, rubbing one's tongue with a sapphire is supposed to make a man both wise and articulate. You might call it an ancient, intellectual blarney stone. One wintry evening when Scrabble and everything else break down you might try placing a sapphire on your tongue for a few minutes to see what that does to your mental apparatus. The possibilities lying about in the game I-rubbed-my-tongue-with-a-sapphire are endless. Sometimes I think they had much more fun in the Middle Ages than we do.

"Did you know the oriental sapphire was so revered by the Greeks, it was dedicated by them to Apollo?" asked one voice, and before I could determine the specific shade of the stone, another voice twittered unbelievingly:

"The King of Ava is supposed to have had a sapphire in his treasury that weighed *nine hundred and fifty-one carats*."

"Where's Ava?" challenged the smallest voice in the room, unimpressed by the size of the jewel. The silence was like the desert at midday until the group historian broke in to promise he would look it up and enlighten us later. I found afterward it was a ruined city in Upper Burma founded in the fourteenth century and destroyed by an earthquake in 1837.

As the discussion continued I learned more and more

about my September sapphire. It was intriguing to find among its legends that it has great powers against poison. If any Virgo has a dear enemy who is hemlock bent, get her hence to the nearest sapphire mine. It may help foil a deadly plot.

Alfred the Great wrote of the sapphire and made some extravagant claims for its efficacy. He claimed that the sapphire cured abscesses and declared he had witnessed *one* sapphire cure *two* abscesses. He also said "the sapphire invigorates the body, induces piety, confirms the mind in goodness, brings about peaceful agreements, cures headaches [*adios* aspirin], checks sweating [likewise Right Guard], makes a man chaste, and cools internal heat." Ah well! One little sapphire can't do everything.

The ruby legends thread themselves through every age. St. Epiphanius of Constantia, who was a fourth century church father, not only averred that rubies shine in the darkness, he also contended they shine through vestments with undiminished fire. Imagine the embarrassment of trying to leave with one of your host's loud-speaking ruby-encrusted goblets under your scarf.

Epiphanius is the man who wrote an allegorical interpretation of the twelve jewels on the breastplate of the high priest Aaron. He also wrote the pamphlet *Against the Images*, undoubtedly an attack against iconoclasm. With such orthodox qualifications behind him, he must have had strong support for his theory that rubies shone through garments.

Gems were an important part of the lives of the men of antiquity. The ancients even believed the ruby held the spark of life. The spiritual as well as the material potency attributed to gems was apparently a primal part of the life of the ancient. A man's fate just might be carried about in the form of a gemstone. Wasn't it Henry V who wore the Black Prince's Ruby into the Battle of Agincourt? And remember what did not happen to him! He won handsomely, but one wonders if he would have felt invincible if he had known then that it was a red spinel he carried instead of a precious ruby talisman. In

any event the "ruby" belonged to the man and the moment
and became part of history with him.

As talk will, we passed from rubies and sapphires to the
gleam of the diamond, and a particular stone that is supposed
to invite ill luck. Although the Hope Diamond is storied with
a history of tragedy, I have always thought the real fixation
people have with this gem is the mystery in its brilliant blue
depths. The Hope Diamond looks more like a sapphire to me
than most sapphires. This is one of the two world-famous
jewels that received the setting it deserved as a frame. Even
the chain that holds it is glorious and brilliantly precious. The
other stone is the Tiffany Yellow Diamond to which I hope to
give a satisfying nod in the chapter on diamonds.

Our host ended our gem ramblings by giving us a final
admonition that sapphires are stones, like the ruby, emerald,
topaz, and garnet, that may be found in placer deposits. This
is an area where quite large stones have been found; so don't
turn your back on residual deposits of heavy minerals in river
beds or by the sea, for those spots just might contain that
egg-sized gemstone you've thirsted for.

The delicious dinner at the charming inn which had faded
into so many tales about rubies and sapphires and other gems
was finally over and we left for our mountain house with at
least one guest considerably more addicted, if possible, to
gems than before the dessert.

Saturday was greeted reluctantly. It seemed prudent not to
plan to go to the mine as there would be too much of a
scramble to dress, mine, and then dress again for the trip back
to New York. I planned to drive to Greenville, South Carolina, to take my train—a pioneer to the end.

It was decided that I would mine vicariously that day, so
some new house guests—cousins of my host—went to the
mine a little after nine o'clock. Around noon they returned,
and the lone gentleman in the group emptied what looked
like one-quarter of a baby's food bottle of gems onto the table
at which I sat.

"He found those at Gibson's," offered my host, reminding

me in a final lesson that nothing is totally lost. Gibson's is the place where we had a fruitless day, no luck at all, because we had gone at the wrong time.

Gibson's had apparently just been bulldozed and our house guest showed four very good-sized rubies and a palmful of sapphires. If he had been there a month he would have needed a barrel to take home his treasures. I wondered for a foolish minute if I could face another week of mining—perhaps, at Gibson's.

9

❧

Gems by Mail

"Out of sight, out of mind," is a cliché I dislike as much as any other chewed-up phrase, but it is the only thing that describes what happened to me when I returned home. I had brought back from North Carolina only one beautiful, polished, cabochon-cut ruby—total value $175—and a mayonnaise jar almost full of not-so-perfect stones, including what I thought and still think might be a diamond—so somehow the entire mining expedition went out of my head. Then, one day, about a month and a half after I returned from Highlands, the postman rang thrice.

With extraordinary dispatch not native to our postman, who considers mail deliveries a social encounter, I was handed a plain box with Archie Jellen's name in the upper left hand corner. I didn't even think what it might be, and then I lifted the crude cardboard cover to reveal some of the most glorious stones I have ever seen. One ruby dazzled up at me as though it could not wait for the lid to be lifted so I could enjoy its lilac-red beauty. I used every high-powered magnifying glass in my den, and in every test the stones were gorgeous. I felt like Croesus, but oddly, the real joy was in the beauty of the stones. It seemed sacrilegious even to mount them into jewelry.

When I showed them around, some of my friends were impressed and wanted to take the next plane for North Carolina. Others looked at them as though they were shirt buttons. I felt like Ranjit Singh, that Lion of the Punjab.

The most unusual encounter involving the gems came when I walked into a famous jewelry store where I have an account and showed them to a man at one of their precious gems counters. I wanted some information on having some of them set.

"Where did you get those?" he asked in the tones of the house detective.

"North Carolina," sez I.

"Hardly," sez he.

"Even money," offered I.

"Let's take them over here," sez he.

"I'm right behind you," sez I.

He brought them over to a gentleman with considerably more disdain on his face.

"We don't set any gems except our own," sez he.

"Not even for a good customer?" asked I.

"Never," sez he, including Michael, the archangel, in his withering refusal.

"What do you suggest?" asks I.

"Some *Madison Avenue* jeweler," sez he, with a lip curl that would make Alexandre perish to imitate it.

As I walked away from the counter I heard the two men arguing, and high eyebrows two was saying to high eyebrows one, "Why did you bring her to *my* counter?" I was enjoying myself hugely in spite of the rejection. There is a delicious feeling when you know you are as innocent as a baby, in being mistaken for a female Raffles.

Incidentally, I recently priced a star ruby in that store of the same shade and, I trust, purity as one of my own and the price was $1,050—and it was only half as large as mine. Small wonder the salesman didn't know what to do with the stranger and her bagful of unset gems. Someone told me afterward the Cowee Valley mine was formerly leased by the jewelry company before World War I.

Most of the stones I mined were cabochon cut. That is a convex form of gem cutting introduced by the Romans, and it is the oldest form of gem cut in use today. The cabochon is the best cut for asterias or star stones. Many of my stones, rubies *and* sapphires, were asteriated—with exquisite starlike patterns. Star stones reflect light from the interior of the gems.

Asterism is caused by minute inclusions in the stone, producing a star with six rays in the ruby and sapphire. You will find usually the star garnet with only four rays, although six rays are possible. Rutile needles or hollow tubes can cause the phenomenon of asterism. The fibrous inclusions in the star stones are regularly arranged about sixty degrees apart. Sapphires are the stones in which you will find the star effect most frequent.

It must be remembered that most gems are not beautiful in their rough form. They must be properly cut and polished to bring out their color and brilliance. The polished star sapphire shows colossal beauty by reflected light, and only by reflected light. The sapphire doesn't light *itself* and it loses much of its brilliance at night. This would not seem to be true of the ruby. It has been said that Noah's only light in the ark was supposed to be that of the carbuncle—and carbuncle in the past meant the ruby as well as the garnet or spinel—so Noah probably saw things by the glow of the ruby fire, as they are alleged to glow in the dark. That legend is a far cry from the way I always pictured things in that old ark. I guess I was turned around by the two-by-two syndrome.

When you are thinking of *your* huge potential star sapphire remember these stones come in remarkably large sizes. A friend of mine in California has a sapphire that is larger than any grape I have ever seen. It is a perfect star, a double star. It weighs 111 carats, and is worth $75,000. She did not mine it, of course—but someone did. The next one that size could be *yours.*

Asteriated stones, especially large ones like my friend's, are unique in that no matter how many star stones you cut from a larger star each of the smaller stones will have the star in it.

They will be almost perfect duplicates of each other as far as asterism is concerned. So don't be afraid to cut or have your whopping star sapphire "find" cut into several smaller stones for your heirs or even for your dearest enemy. There will be enough for everyone, but be awfully certain whoever cuts the stone knows exactly *how* it is done.

Since we have said the red spinel has been mistaken for the more valuable ruby (remember the Black Prince's Ruby) it might be a good idea to say a word or twenty about spinel so you won't think the gemologist has cheated you when he shatters you with the news, "no-it-is-not-a-ruby."

When spinel is pure, like corundum, it is devoid of color. Stones of this type are very rare, however, as are most pure mineral stones. The balas ruby is one of the two kinds of red spinel valued as a gem. It is a rosy-red variety and derives its name from Balascia, the ancient name for Badakhshan, the area from which the best stones were brought in the Middle Ages. Besides the shades of red, spinel comes in orange (called rubicelle), blue, violet (when the purple tones are very pronounced this is called almandine spinel), and other hues.

Spinel often occurs in close association with corundum, but it is an oxide of aluminum and magnesium and is *unrelated to ruby*. Such similarities are good reasons for realizing you cannot trust your own eye and must depend on a gemologist to tell you the true nature of the stones you have mined. Don't feel too insecure, though, if you find you have a balas ruby or red spinel instead of a real ruby. If the gracious Queen of England can wear a gem of red spinel in her crown without flinching, there is no disgrace in your wearing one the size of a walnut to the next office picnic. Incidentally, the Black Prince's Ruby is very, very lovely. I don't know how it could be improved in beauty if it had the mineral properties of the real ruby.

The Timur Ruby, also in the British royal regalia, is spinel too, and its uncut 361 carats are nothing for even the Queen to apologize for. Although it is uncut, it *has* been polished. This is a stone which also came into the possession of Ranjit Singh of Lahore. He coddled the Koh-i-noor Diamond for some time as well. There is a man I would like to have followed about just to know how he acquired all those lovely gemstones. The Timur Ruby was apparently named after the Amir Timur to whom its history dates—back to the late fourteenth century. He is the conqueror Tamerlane who seized the stone in the capture of Delhi in 1398. This lovely jewel was celebrated throughout the Orient as the Tribute of the World, and is the largest stone of its kind in existence.

There are differences of opinion sometimes as to what is a pink sapphire and what is a pink ruby, but you have the assurance of most experts that when corundum is pale and pink it is usually called a sapphire. There is a salmon-orange hue to the pink sapphire that is never found in the ruby.

Rubies and sapphires are distinguished by carats, the stand-ard weight measure of all precious stones, one carat being one-fifth of a gram. Carat is a word that had its origins in the seed of the carob tree. The seeds of that tree were so uniform in weight they were used for weighing gems far back in antiq-uity.

The sapphire does not have the fantastic rarity and worth of the perfect ruby and although it is the same mineral sub-stance it does not graduate in value at the same rate. No other stone increases in value *in proportion to increase in weight as does a ruby*. The more one studies the ruby the more one realizes not only its artistic but also its intrinsic worth. Rubies of first quality are rarer than diamonds and consequently more valuable than diamonds of corresponding grade. A per-fect five carat ruby will be double the price of a diamond of the same weight, and a ruby of ten carats would be triple the price of a diamond of the same weight and perfection. A perfect ruby is considered one of the rarest of nature's produc-tions.

The times and circumstances dictate which gem will be the

most valuable. Today, the emerald is the most valued, and although the diamond is more plentiful than some other stones it has been so carefully controlled and so discriminately exploited it follows the emerald in value. This does not discount what we have said about the ruby, but that applies to the larger, perfect stones, which are rarities.

I was interested to read that because Thailand rubies are darker in color there is quite a distinction made between Thai and Burmese rubies. I mention that because my own North Carolina rubies were mistaken at a glance for Burmese rubies by an eminent gemologist. Thailand is distinguished, however, as the home of glorious sapphires and produces more than half the world's supply. Green corundum has also been found there.

Ceylon has an abundance of sapphires, but rubies are rare there—although one may find magnificent yellow corundum, which has been called oriental topaz and which the Ceylonese call king topaz. I have a Ceylon sapphire in a ring whose setting far outstrips the paleness of the stone. The designer of the ring was so talented that even a pebble put in that setting would have been enhanced. It is seldom that anyone can make the frame so entrancing that the picture is minimal. In this case a pale, cloudy sapphire has been given princely treatment. That is how important setting is to a gem. Cutting is even more crucial.

Each stone is different. The person you entrust it to must *know* stones and if he is not always certain he must have deep instincts about gems. There is just as much genius and skill required in gem cutting as in creating an outstanding piece of sculpture. *Any* wrong turn is costly.

A "diamond cutter" is always called just that. He generally specializes in no other stones but the diamond. All other gem cutters are lapidaries. Diamonds are cut to expose *their brilliancy*, which is their main beauty; other gems are usually cut to reveal *their color*. The tools of lapidaries are not complicated; the important thing is getting the utmost in beauty and value from the rough stone.

It is the gem cutter who can make your stone a better or a lesser gem. If he does not know his craft superbly, he will not minimize waste, and although you might get a beautiful setting it could cost you more than it needed to in loss of gem weight. The surer and more impeccable the gem cutter's judgment the more valuable your stone.

It has been said the Koh-i-noor Diamond was nearly ruined, and depreciated in value and beauty, when it was recut for Queen Victoria to an allegedly shallow brilliant of approximately 108 carats from the 186 carats it weighed in its Indian form. Of course, since it is still valued at something like a half-million dollars I can't say tears for it are in order. Of all the gems I have seen, this is the most glorious; and to my mind the additional cutting made it lovelier. But, more about that in the chapter on diamonds.

When you have mined, don't hesitate to talk out the possibilities for your stones and don't gallop off to a quick decision as to what to do with them. The longer you keep the cut and polished stones in your Riker Mount (those cardboard, shallow boxes with glass covers) the longer you will have to think about their possibilities, and you will be growing in gem knowledge and able to speak more intelligently when you approach a gemologist or jewelry designer. Later chapters in this book will give you hints on many, many things you can do with your stones. Most of the large sapphires in the world have come from the Orient. The British Museum of Natural History has an image of Buddha cut out of a single Indian sapphire mounted on a gold pin. It is an exquisite little jewel that suggests many more things can be done with gems than one thinks of initially.

The world's supply of good rubies comes from the well-known mines near Mogok in Upper Burma about four thousand feet above sea level. Although some stones are found there in the limestone on the sides of the hills, most occur in the alluvial deposits—in the river beds. While the Burmese mines are known to be very old their beginnings are as hazy as the first days of some of the world's most famous gems or the legends that have attached themselves to them. How I wish I could see the Shwe Dagon Pagoda of Rangoon over which a banner floated, studded with precious gems worth one million dollars, many of them rubies.

But one never knows where she will run into a star ruby. I have so many interests I am always looking down someone's throat or following an oddity down the road. One day I was late for an appointment and leaped into a taxicab carrying the only soundless driver in all of this city. I was working on something in my corner of the cab and paid no attention to him until we arrived at my destination. As we stopped I looked up and noticed the hand he had raised to shut off the meter. I could hardly believe what I saw. He was wearing a ruby in his ring that almost made my eyes water.

"Is it a real ruby?" I asked, not trusting my own judgment at all, at all. His mouth broke into a smile that ran from one side of his face to the other.

"Just step outside the cab and look at this star," he invited. As he thrust his hand out of the cab window the ruby looked hazy pink but still very large.

"It's a *gemstone*." He accented the word. "You are standing in its light," he chided. I stepped aside and let the sun hit it, and the most fantastic miracle took place on that very expensive hand. The cloudy note in the ruby disappeared and the most finely etched, perfect, six-radii star appeared that I ever hope to see.

"It's a gemstone," he repeated, as I was paying him. "It's worth twenty thousand dollars," he told me proudly. "It's from my better days." All I could think of was the thirty-five-cent tip I had just given him.

Hopefully, many questions may be answered in subsequent pages, in chapters dealing with individual stones more specifically or pin-pointed areas of mining.

When you consider the lions, tigers, and other elements man had to fight long ago in the East Indian jungles to get to precious rubies you have to be grateful to the Wright Brothers, who made it possible for you to get to your favorite mining site in a few hours.

I have every intention of one day finding a ruby as large as a dragon's egg and as beautiful as a sunrise. Meanwhile, it is nice to think of putting a ruby in every wine goblet one owns and inviting all the special people in one's life to visit and drink vin rosé above the ruby rays. It seems the ruby will always be considered a precious stone. It is inconceivable there will be a day when a queen won't want a ruby in her crown or a prince won't give a band of rubies to his princess. Somehow, the very name, ruby, even more than emerald or diamond, stirs thoughts of blazing gems and titillating tradition. If you get bored with the stone, if your interest flags just a little bit, just remember the Subah of Deccan wore it as an armlet—and you can too.

We can't promise that you will find a ruby as large or as pure as the ruby of the sovereign of Pegu, whose gemstone initiated the proverb of ruby purity, but you will have more fun than you have ever had in your life as you begin to see those little gems trickle into your jar and know one of them *could* be a match for the gem that rested so long ago in Pegu.

The very important thing to remember is that this country is alive with gemstones from one end to the other. There are gems for the taking in every one of the fifty states. But you are most likely to find rubies and sapphires in the following places:

NORTH CAROLINA—You should find both ruby and sapphire there, especially in Franklin, Macon, and Clay counties. Haywood and Iredell counties have some good sapphires. Cashiers in Jackson County has both ruby and sapphire.

WASHINGTON—There are a few shades of sapphire at Okanogan County.

GEORGIA—Try Towns County. Rabun County has some red corundum. There should be ruby in Habersham County at Alexander Mountain.

MONTANA—This state is celebrated for its sapphires, as

Yogo Gulch will reveal. The counties of Silver Bow, Powell, Granite, Deer Lodge, Judith Basin, and Custer have sapphire. Lewis and Clark County (Helena) has both ruby and sapphire.

IDAHO—This state has both ruby and sapphire. You may find only sapphire at Nez Perce. Try Adams County for the ruby.

ALABAMA—Coosa County has corundum.

MASSACHUSETTS—Salem has corundum.

NEW JERSEY—Franklin has sapphire, and you may find some ruby there. Also try Sparta.

ALASKA—Has some ruby and sapphire—but you are more likely to find gold there. You may find star ruby and star sapphire in southeastern Alaska, however. Try Copper River Juneau Indian Reservation.

INDIANA—Has some sapphire. You might explore Morgan County. You could stumble on some garnet or zircon there too.

WYOMING—Fremont County has sapphire and ruby.

CALIFORNIA—You will find corundum in Riverside County, along with spinel, topaz, rose quartz, and a host of other gemstones.

PENNSYLVANIA—Try Delaware County and Unionville in Chester County.

COLORADO—You might explore Chaffee County there.

SOUTH CAROLINA—Cherokee County has sapphire—also Anderson County.

If you are looking for Canadian sites to mine, write to the Geological Survey of Canada at Ottawa, Ontario, which should be able to direct you to the many stones available in Canada. However, you might find sapphire at Stony Lake, Peterborough County, Ontario.

Gems are some of the most expressive voices of civilization. They are a memento of the past, making us realize that we must make use of the best things of yesterday to enhance our present and future. They are banners of elegance, brilliants that light a new day for us. They have been forming, some of them, for millions of years, and even the primitive Indians responded to their lure. How little we can afford to take their history or their beauty for granted.

The ruby is my own charming lantern, lighting the way to many more adventures than its clay beginnings would suggest. From its rosiest shade to deepest carmine the ruby is a queen of gems.

If *you* would wear a ruby on every finger—and multiple rings on any or every finger belong to our age—throw away your mundanities and leave with your knapsack for, at least, North Carolina. You can't guess how many treasures are buried in the ground waiting for your little spade.

10

❧

What Else but a Diamond!

Diamonds are far less plentiful in the United States than rubies, but since more than 100,000 gemstones have already been found in Arkansas it is not too optimistic to presume they are to be found if one takes the trouble to look for them.

As gems, diamonds are the simplest of all stones in chemical composition. They are pure carbon. One of the oddities of the chemical composition of a diamond is that as pure carbon it is the same as graphite. It would seem no two elements were ever further removed from each other. Graphite (from the Greek *graphein*, to write), a dull and loosely crystallized earthy form of carbon, is black and soft enough to be used in lead pencils, while the diamond, a compactly crystallized carbon, is the hardest of all minerals and brilliant, especially when faceted perfectly. A diamond may be converted to graphite by exposing it to a very high temperature while excluding air. Many diamond treasures were sacrificed in experiments made through the ages to test the combustibility of diamonds. They *are* combustible, needless to say.

The diamond, the hardest substance known to man, is immeasurably harder than corundum (ruby and sapphire). It has been reported to be from 10 to 140 times harder. Only a diamond can cut a diamond. Although corundum, as we have said, is shown as 9 on Mohs' Scale of Hardness, the distance between the hardness of the ruby and the sapphire and the diamond, which is shown as 10, is indeed appreciable. Nothing, dear hearts, including your flinthearted landlord, is harder than this famous gem.

The diamond was named that because the ancients felt it was invincible. Much like our word "adamant," the diamond gave way to nothing. However, in spite of its hardness, it can be reduced by shattering or heat, and a hard blow can crack it. One must be careful with diamonds, as with any precious thing, and they should be kept scrupulously clean.

Although there are about six ways to reach diamonds, we will continue to explore the surface mining possibilities—which are alluvial—and pit mining, and only those in North America. The majority of gems are mined from gem gravels and not from their primary source, in any event. Mining for diamonds can be quite different from a ruby hunt. For instance you can pan for diamonds in the Great Lakes region. Diamonds can be found in the beds of streams, when dry especially, because they are great travelers due to their durability and can roam far from their beginnings. Where other stones would disintegrate and perish, the diamond rubs and tumbles itself into possible further beauty. The Great Lakes area would be a natural place to find diamonds as they are a heavy mineral that is *frequently* found in placer deposits, remaining when softer stones are swept along the river beds. Diamonds may also be washed up by the sea.

However, diamond pipes are the only source rock of diamonds. Diamond pipe is diamond-bearing rock. Scientists hesitate to place the exact origin of diamonds but they do say that nature has been in preparation for this stone for millions of years. Talking to someone at the Museum of Natural History in New York, I was awed to hear him toss out little unrecent dates like "two hundred million years ago" in relation to the beginnings of diamond pipes. That's not terribly old if the findings of a South African scientist are true, and the world really is four billion years old and not just two billion as previously thought.

I have been told that some of the best diamonds recovered

in this country have been found in Cleveland County, North Carolina, although the largest diamond ever found in the United States is the Uncle Sam Diamond, owned by Peikin, formerly of Fifth Avenue in New York. It was mined at Murfreesboro, Arkansas. Originally 40.23 carats, it was cut to an emerald cut of 12.42 carats—its present form. According to Mr. B. Beryl Peikin, it is worth about $250,000 today. Found in 1924, it is $13/16$ of an inch by $7/16$ of an inch.

The largest Murfreesboro recent find is the Star of Arkansas Diamond, found by Mrs. A. L. Parker of Dallas, Texas, a rock hound. The stone was 15.31 carats and cut to a marquise brilliant of 8.27 carats. Someone who saw this particular diamond says it was slipper-shaped and very fine. He described it as looking like pure spring water. Its original shape presented cutting problems, however.

Arkansas, by the way, *has the volcanic rock that pressures diamonds to the surface.* Diamonds, which need extremely high pressures for their formation, are driven to the surface by volcaniclike processes. They occur in kimberlite, an igneous rock, are formed at depth and carried to the surface through gas pressure explosions. Arkansas is the only place in the United States where diamonds are mined from original rocks. In Pike County, Arkansas, the diamonds are in peridotite, an important igneous rock of which kimberlite is a variety. Generally, however, diamonds are found in alluvial deposits. California and the Eastern United States have glacial deposits, a possible resting place for the gems. Doesn't that excite you into thinking you can own a personally mined diamond almost too blissfully vulgar to wear to church?

The stories of diamond finds, especially on the African continent, make one think some truly great diamond treasures must be lurking around *our* shores too. Hans Merenskey, who also discovered platinum on Merenskey Reef, filled a preserve jar with diamonds that were washed up on the South African coast. According to D. M. V. Manson of the Museum of Natural History in New York, there are remote possibilities for diamond mining on the east coast of North America from the Monteregian Hills in Montreal to Alabama, as these have volcanic features related to kimberlite rock, which, as we said, is the matrix (mother rock) of diamonds.

Most diamonds are not particularly alluring in their rough form, and the great difficulty is in recognizing them. As a matter of fact they are seldom recognized instantly. Greasy and pebble-toned they are unlikely "specimens." It takes a very trained eye to know a diamond is really a diamond—even at a second glance. Many pairs of trained eyes have been wrong in detecting rough diamonds through the ages.

The identification of diamonds is one area in which the "rock hound" has an advantage over the "gem hound." A rock hound will pick up a stone that *might* be interesting, and it *could* be a diamond, but the gem hound will discriminate against anything that does not look like gem gravel and probably overlook the unappealing rough diamond. There is often a gray film, like onion skin, over the diamond that rubbing and polishing wear away, revealing some of its beauty. However, it is not until the diamond has been properly cut that its brilliance is exposed. The refractory element of the diamond must be coddled. The brilliant cut with its precise arrangement of fifty-eight facets produces exquisite and maximum brilliance.

It is hard to believe there are more than two hundred recognized shades of white diamond. If one considers the diamond statistics however, he might feel only a slim hope of ever finding a diamond. In South Africa, the home of ninety-two percent of the diamond output of the world, it has been said it takes twenty tons of rock and gravel to produce four carats of diamonds and less than two of those carats will be suitable for cutting as gems.

Diamonds are found in what is called blue ground or blue rock, in matrix that is hard, a peculiar formation with a gray-blue cast. Imagine penetrating tons of blue ground (it looks quite yellow-toned at the surface, incidentally) to find one carat of diamond. It is easier to go to Arkansas and surface dig there, I can tell you.

Try to find out what the condition of the gravel is when you arrive at your digging or mining site. If it is an area on which tons of earth have just been dropped you aren't likely to find anything there if you mine for a month. ALWAYS TRY TO GO WHEN THE CIRCUMSTANCES ARE BEST FOR THE EXPOSURE OF NEW GEM GRAVEL.

In mining for diamonds in the Great Lakes region, for instance, you will probably find them as glacial deposits. Don't expect to know a diamond the minute you see one. As I have explained, they look more like slippery pebbles. Try to find out everything you can about a rough and a finished diamond before you begin to hunt for one.

I discovered one particular thing about gemology and gem hounds or rock hounds generally. Everyone has a different idea about various phases of the hobby or science, whichever way he is pursuing it, and opinions are strong, firm, and, not surprisingly, conflicting. I have frequently felt like a ping-pong ball in turning left and right between experts' opinions.

One should read this book with the thought that many things have been said about gems, and the more one knows about gems and the more avenues he can walk to pursue them the better are the chances of finding a superior gemstone. It is worth a pause here to say this is a book of incidental gemstone knowledge, designed merely to interest more people in a rewarding hobby and point them a bit more directly toward a new, exciting adventure.

For instance, no source of diamonds has been more talked about than the so-called diamond mines of Golconda. However, the "diamonds of Golconda" were brought not from the fortress of Golconda but from the mines of Raolconda and other localities situated in the territory of the Golconda kings. Golconda has so often been called a "fabled mine," perhaps there is a truth to that after all . . . Golconda *is* a fable.

I shudder when I think of some of the things people have

done in their quest for diamonds, and their stealth to secrete them. Many of the tales we have had handed down to us grew out of the great experiences of a man by the name of Jean Baptiste Tavernier, a gem merchant and French traveler. He is one of the people who visited the diamond mines of the Golconda district and published a description of them and the method of working them. Tavernier was on a commission for Louis XIV so he had access to many places others could not penetrate. Also, he had a reputation for meticulous honesty among the royal princes and rulers he visited so their doors were thrown wide open to him.

It is this seventeenth-century gem merchant, who left us so many memoirs about jewels around the world, who tells about the slave miner who forced a diamond into a corner of his eye so perfectly he completely concealed the gem. I can't help but agree with Cervantes, who said "Every tooth in a man's head is more valuable than a diamond," and think that someone's values went a bit awry in India that day.

Golconda, the home area of the famous Koh-i-noor, and undoubtedly of the Blue Hope Diamond as well, is situated between Bombay and Madras. When you remember that sixty thousand men were employed at Golconda in 1665 and that the field is now abandoned you realize what a small part of the world's diamond flow India now controls. The mines known as Golconda appear to have been exhausted by the end of the seventeenth century, and have yielded little during the time they have been worked since then.

The largest diamond ever found is the Cullinan Diamond, which in its rough form weighed 3,106 carats. Found in the Premier Mines near Pretoria in the Transvaal by an employee, Frederick Wells, on an inspection tour, the gem was named after Thomas A. Cullinan, who was the chairman of the Premier Diamond Company. It appears somewhat unfair that the man who discovered it originally was not recognized by having *his* name awarded to the gem.

The Cullinan, which was found at the turn of this century,

was sent to Amsterdam to be cut, three years after Mr. Wells stumbled over it. The largest stone cut from it, the Star of Africa (reputed to be the largest and most perfect diamond in the world) is 530.2 carats and is in the royal scepter of the Queen of England. Since the Cullinan Diamond was given to the British crown, all the other diamonds cut from this fabulous stone—eight large stones and ninety-six small brilliants—are also part of the royal regalia. These include the 317.4 carat Second Star of Africa, now in the Imperial State Crown of England, the Third Star of Africa, which weighs 94.45 carats, and a fourth large stone of 63.45 carats. I would recommend that they put the latter stone in Queen Mary's crown in place of the piece of quartz or whatever it is that debases it at the moment.

I was prepared to dislike the huge Star of Africa that was cut from the Cullinan, and had the feeling intensified after I saw an unlovely model of it in the gemstone collection of the Geological Museum in London. Then I saw the stone itself in the royal scepter and almost genuflected before it. The long months of cutting and faceting the largest white diamond in the world had exposed its maximum beauty. It is a staggering sight, lighting the royal scepter of England into a treasure worthy to be held by any monarch. The stone is called a pendeloque and weighs just under a quarter of a pound. It took less than a year to complete the work of cutting and faceting the largest diamond ever found.

The Second Star of Africa is very beautiful too, and sitting as it does just under the Black Prince's Ruby in the Imperial Crown of State of Elizabeth II one is struck by the marvelous wedding of the uncut but polished spinel and the meticulously faceted diamond.

When one considers the gems, the diamonds that came out of the near-fabled mine areas such as Golconda, our little mining successes today seem slight indeed. The Koh-i-noor, which is in the crown of the Queen Mother of England, traces back to the fourteenth century specifically, although tales about it take it back to the tenth century. Koh-i-noor means "mountain of light." Its original weight was reputed to be an impressive eight hundred carats. It was cut in the nineteenth century to a mere 108 carats, which is its present weight. It had been 186 carats in its Indian form and when Ranjit Singh of Lahore possessed it. When it was recut for Queen Victoria to a "shallow" brilliant of 108 carats (and I can't conceive of any gem weighing 108 carats being shallow), it was said to have lost much of its beauty and long-time glamor. I can tell you it has not. Incidentally, it *is* the private property of the English royal family.

The Koh-i-noor, which was originally found by a sheep-herder, was named for a startled exclamation after the big stone itself had been known to exist for hundreds of years without a name. During the sack of Delhi by the Persians in 1739, Nadir Shah, the conqueror, knew that somewhere in the city he would find the storied great diamond that had been in the peacock throne of Persia. A beauty of the harem told him that the diamond was hidden in a most unlikely place—in the turban of the vanquished Mogul sultan. But how to get the white silk turban with which no Mogul ruler would part any more than an emperor would hand over his crown. Nadir Shah, however, tricked the enemy into exchanging turbans with him during a feast. Then, rushing to his own tent, he began to unroll the yards and yards of silk. When the great gem, then 186 carats in its old Indian cut, rolled out on the carpet at the feet of Nadir Shah, he exclaimed "Koh-i-noor!" as it was indeed a mountain-of-light.

Of all the gems I have seen in my life, this is the most breathtakingly beautiful stone the world could possibly hold. It is set with great vision and taste in the crown of Queen Elizabeth, the Queen Mother of England, and it is surrounded by diamonds from a circlet that had been worn by Queen Victoria. I understand this diamond, the Koh-i-noor, is supposed to bring good luck to the woman who wears it, but ill luck to the man.

Colored diamonds receive a great deal of acclamation, and most of them deserve it. You may find them in blue, yellow, brown, red, violet, pink, or black. But these colored diamonds are surprisingly rare. The rarest of all colored diamonds is a red one. The gem treasure I most yearned to see, at one time, was the ruby-red 10-carat diamond called Paul I, which was part of the Russian crown jewels. Of course, I was prepared to discover that it was spinel. I was not too long in finding out the sorry facts. The very authoritative Robert Crowningshield of the Gemological Institute of America told me the stone is in fact not red but pink-toned and has had its color intensified with "backing." So much for Paul I, only important to me now as the son of Catherine the Great.

I knew for a certainty that the Koh-i-noor and the Cullinan are "for real." When I suggested to a guard in the Tower of London, where the crown jewels of England are kept, that I had been advised on unimpeachable authority the real Koh-i-noor was elsewhere and the gem on view was only a model, he almost lost his British cool. "Madam, I *know* that is the real Koh-i-noor Diamond, and I shall stake my life on it," he thrust at me. He didn't have to go that far because the glories of the stone dazzled up at me in a language no other stone could possibly speak. I kept the memory of its beauty with me long after I had ridden away from the Jewel House of London Tower!

The Tiffany Yellow, an African stone, is one of the loveliest of all colored diamonds, and one of the most beautifully mounted. Its weight is 128.7 carats and it measures 2½ by 2½ inches, but it doesn't look oversized as do so many large, famous gems. This is a diamond that has had all the best handling (Jean Schlumberger set it), and the result is a yellow diamond of imperishable beauty. It is valued at over half a million dollars.

When one remembers that the Hope Diamond has been recut, and was even larger when it rested in the Golden Fleece of Louis XV in the eighteenth century, one can only be awed by this "unlucky" blue stone. The Hope Diamond, as already stated, is blue, and forty-four carats of dazzling brilliance. Bought by Henry Thomas Hope in the early part of the nineteenth century, it belonged to the Hope family until it was sold to the Sultan of Turkey. Later it became the much discussed possession of Evelyn Walsh McLean of Washington, D.C. In spite of the fact that it is a gem purported to have a history of bad luck for its owner, the Hope Diamond could always find a willing buyer. After the death of Mrs. McLean, Harry Winston, a New York jeweler, bought it and much later presented it to the Smithsonian Institution, where it now rests as one of that museum's most prized displays.

When a diamond is apple-green and faultless, weighs more than forty carats and costs less than $50,000, even in the eighteenth century, it sounds like the biggest bargain of the diamond legends to me. Augustus the Strong (undoubtedly why he got it for that price), purchased it. It *was* in the Green Vaults of Dresden but I believe the winds of chance or politics had moved it elsewhere. However, someone told me recently it has been returned. I saw a model of the Dresden Green Diamond, and it is gorgeous in color and in cutting. It has always been mounted in a shoulder knot (a pendant type ornament) as part of the Saxon Regalia. But, if one must stumble onto a bargain tale let it be the kind that surrounds the Tuscany Yellow Diamond. This gem was supposedly bought at a street stall in Florence as a bit of yellow quartz. Although it was considered to be "blemished" with its faint traces of yellow, it weighed almost 134 carats. Formerly the property of the Grand Dukes of Tuscany, it was later owned by the Emperor of Austria.

Although colored diamonds, especially red and blue hues, are very rare, we know they can be found. The lasting beauty of the large Hope Diamond, with its inscrutable blue eye, and even the Paul I Diamond, that nearly ruby-red treasure, are available to tease us with some of the delights the earth holds. To keep one's enthusiasms close to reality it must be said that the number of diamonds of the first water which exceed one hundred carats in weight *are* rare indeed, but you can stumble upon diamond treasure in odd places, and right in some of our fifty states, as we have shown.

Here are some additional tidbits about diamonds, including some by Dorothy Dignam, a feature writer and a gem historian who has many interesting tales to relate. Much of the lore about the ill omens connected with gems was started by the gem owners themselves. The background on how tales of violence and death came to be associated with the great diamonds again goes back to the Indian rulers. They had no insurance policies, no trigger alarms, no electric eyes to protect their jewels so they invented stories of dire misfortune and sudden death that could strike a slave or attendant who even touched a diamond. As a further precaution, the most valuable stones would be hidden in a different place each day. A thief might be apprehended just seeking out the new hiding place. (See the chapter on amethysts for a recent accursed gem.)

When the citadel of Golconda in central India fell to the Moguls in 1687, the invaders rolled out forty-eight huge jars which contained the water supply of the besieged. Soldiers were ordered to empty the water, and in one great jug were thousands of diamonds and gold coins—in perfect condition. That's enough to make anyone give up wine and look for new waterways.

The diamond does have one ancient superstition that delights me. IT WAS CONSIDERED A PROTECTION AGAINST GHOSTS. What better reason for pinning that gorgeous brooch to your p.j.'s—especially since the white ones are likely to prowl after dark. Of course the legend about the diamonds and ghosts will never replace the most intriguing tidbit I have uncovered about the powers of gemstones. The carbuncles (you remember they used to call rubies and garnets, as well as spinel, carbuncles) *were supposed to have the power to make their wearer invisible*. If it is true their wearer was indeed invisible and the carbuncle was alleged to have shone in the dark, meeting such a phenomenon must have been a shattering minute for anyone facing it. Unlike Albertus Magnus, who witnessed the cure of two abscesses by one single sapphire, I have been unable to unearth any proof but only hearsay that such a thing as invisibility ever happened. I am willing to believe it, though, until someone disproves it to me, because the delightful stories behind gemstones add such a fascinating dimension to gemology—and to life.

While it is true that one may swallow the lore (the lively tales of the hopes and promises and the powers of gemstones), when gems are offered as oral medicine it is not so easy to digest *that*. It is said that Lorenzo de Medici was given a dose of powdered diamonds and pearls. While it would be the essence of chic to tonic oneself with precious gems, powdered or unpowdered, and while it might be a great dinner conversation piece, one gets the feeling she would not be around for many more dinners after dining on that fare. Even a pope, Clement VII, is said to have swallowed uncountable powdered potions of gemstones during his last years, which is probably why they were his last.

It is so easy for life to be an adventure "it wonders me," as the Amish say, how anyone finds it dismal, ever, especially with so many lurking treasures in abundance. I have a friend, Tillie Lewis, who is the founder of a fifty-million-dollar food company, Tillie Lewis Foods, now part of the huge billion-dollar Ogden Corporation. She has one of the most beautiful brooches I have ever seen. It is made from two identical marquise yellow diamonds. She is as feminine as lace and she doesn't keep her beautiful stones wrapped away from her own pleasure. She wears her gorgeous pin to breakfast. She sees nothing unusual in putting a pair of flawless yellow diamonds worth $100,000 where someone else would put a bow. After all she *has* the yellow diamonds. She is in love with her husband—she is also a husband pleaser—*ergo*, she is as delightful in her mystery-of-gems mood in the morning as she is under the public lights of a very dress-up charity ball. With her rose-gold hair and huge brown eyes, the yellow diamonds, which were set in Paris by Cartier, are an exquisite touch. Gems should be *worn* when one has them. They should make you feel cherished, force you to look over the picket fence toward bronze doors and pearls in a wine cup. Oh, yes, Tillie Lewis has a white diamond, a pure diamond crystal on her watch. How else can a woman of impeccable gem taste tell when the three-minute eggs are ready to be rescued from a hard boil?

Dorothy Dignam, whose stories of gems never seem to run down, relates that in India, the shahs and princes, who were a superstitious group, called to their stewards for certain gems from their treasury to wear on specific days or during auspicious phases of the moon. Many old diamonds bore "moon" names, such as Moon of the Mountains. The rajah, after consulting his soothsayers, would demand that the Moon of the Mountains be brought to him for wearing on an upper armband on his right arm, the limb of regal authority. There's an idea for fashions in diamonds right there. Incidentally, the Moon of the Mountains is another stone of the Russian crown, which paid an enormous price for it. It was also captured by Nadir Shah at Delhi.

One of the most impressive diamonds of history is the Great Mogul, which is 279 carats but looks larger than that. It resembles a giant, faceted dome. I defy any hand to wear that stone. It is rose cut; and I remember Dorothy Dignam saying that particular type of cutting resembled a gumdrop. The Great Mogul does look somewhat like an oversized version of the candy.

The Cullinan Diamond (incidentally, in the rough, this stone, large though it was, did not look as though so many large and small stones could be cut from it as indeed were) is not the only stone that wasn't called after its finder. The Searcy Diamond, now called the Arkansas Diamond, was discovered by a ten-year-old girl called Pellie. However, there never was a Pellie Diamond because possibly only Pellie herself, as she became older, believed it might be a diamond. A jeweler in nearby Searcy, Arkansas, later encouraged her to send it to the geology department of the University of Arkansas. Tiffany bought the rough stone in the 1940s, but the Searcy name stuck although some identification cards now read "Arkansas Diamond," according to Miss Dignam.

One of the most famous tales of a diamond necklace linked with someone who never owned it concerned the *Queen's Necklace*. This piece of jewelry was a long-distance reason why Queen Marie Antoinette, quite innocent in the affair, literally, ultimately lost her head. One would have expected such a piece of mischief to be at least beautiful or a work of art in some manner. Actually, pictures I have seen of the paste replica of the necklace show it to be as boring as a black onyx ring. But it did contain 500 diamonds, and there are those who have found it inexpressibly appealing probably because its worth today would be four million dollars.

The necklace was originally ordered for Madame du Barry by Louis XV, who, unfortunately, died before it was delivered. Louis XVI, like many husbands before and after him, resisted manfully and refused to buy the necklace because he thought it too costly. His wife, Marie Antoinette, let the matter rest there.

A mischievous female—a milliner according to Carlyle and a lady of the court according to others—suggested to Cardinal de Rohan, who was out of favor with the Queen, that he might again please her if he undertook a secret mission for her. The mission was described as one in which the cardinal would bring the necklace to the Queen without the King's knowledge. The lady, Countess de La Motte, did not tell the cardinal that the Queen herself did not know about the matter. In any event the cardinal obtained the necklace, gave it to a courier whom he thought to be an envoy of the Queen, and *voilà*—man and necklace became temporarily invisible.

The man made off with the jewels and everyone in the

affair seemed to be black with guilt, especially the most innocent party, the Queen. Although Marie Antoinette never
owned the necklace and never plotted to have it, many feel
the extravagance which surfaced could have been another
taper in lighting the fires of a revolution that saw the little
Queen lose her head.

To move on to sweeter scenes, it is fascinating to find that
sugar might be used in making synthetic diamonds. Synthetic
gems must have the same chemical composition as real gems
(synthetic diamonds must have carbon) and the synthetic
source of carbon could be sugar.

While we are talking about diamonds that are not really
diamonds we might mention the best known of these, the
so-called Herkimer Diamonds. Herkimer Diamonds are famous, but they are *not* diamonds. They are quartz crystals—
rock crystals—with the local name of Herkimer Diamonds or
Little Falls Diamonds. They are found, and still are available,
near Little Falls and Middleville in Herkimer County, New
York. Similar rock crystals are found near Hot Springs, Arkansas. They are also scattered in North Carolina and California.

The Cape May Diamond from Cape May, New Jersey, as
well as the Pecos Diamonds of Roswell, Chaves County, New
Mexico—found in the Pecos River—are both very attractive,
colorless crystalline quartz too. This lovely rock crystal, although it lacks the higher brilliance of the diamond, can be
faceted into extraordinary jewelry.

The zircon is another stone that could be mistaken at a
glance for a diamond—unless one were aware of the ability of
this stone to be faceted into a very good substitute for the
more costly gem. The zircon, of course, is considerably more
brittle than the diamond, that hard, hard beauty of the mines
and the streams.

A friend at the British Museum of Natural History showed
me a stone he personally believes *has* the fire of the diamond.
It is called taaffeite. I saw it in a pale mauve shade cut to
about two and a half carats. My friend told me there are only

six authenticated stones of this variety in the world. An expert I know said taaffeite has no more fire than spinel, to which it is closely related. Taaffeite was named after Count Taaffe of Ireland who first suspected it to be a new mineral.

The diamond disperses light to such an extent that it seems multi-hued. It is the true rainbow of gems. But I have seen diamonds that are almost opaque—brown, pink, yellow, and green as well as black. The transparency range of diamonds is wide. I have come across cloudy white diamonds that have closely resembled opals.

When a ray of light strikes the top facet of a diamond, part of the ray is reflected and part is refracted or bent into the stone. The part entering is then dispersed or refracted in color rays and accounts for the rainbow hues of the brilliant gem. The colorless variety is the richest diamond in the flashing of prismatic hues. In some *colored* diamonds the prismatic hues are hardly apparent. Yellow-tinged stones, however, are sometimes more brilliant in artificial light than the colorless diamond, although the diamond does excel all other natural white stones in color dispersion as it gives off every hue of the spectrum, a rare rainbow of brilliance. It is one of the more esoteric pastimes, both rewarding and dazzling, to study a diamond as rays from all directions are bent toward the center of the gem and reflected back through the top.

I have seen diamonds and garnets together in diamond gravel along with some quartz that could confuse any collector. I must say the diamond crystals I have seen in blue ground, however, are quite recognizable as possible diamonds. But, one rough diamond I saw somewhere in my travels looked like a glazed poor ruby, reminding me that diamonds do pass into "bort"—that rather ugly, industrial diamond variety.

It seems like putting a large pin in a very thin balloon, but it must be said: Most of the world's great diamonds have or have had imperfections. I guess it is like oversized fowl—it can be tough. The most beautiful diamond in the world was flawed, but we will penetrate that aspect of the Koh-i-noor Diamond as we explore the importance of proper cutting by exactly the right expert.

It is not an easy thing to remove a diamond flaw completely, so the faceting sometimes must fall just short of genius. The Orloff Diamond had a groovelike flaw. To cut it out completely would have diminished the size of the stone to almost wasted proportions, so the stone was ROSE-CUT and *the flaw was polished* to the same high luster as the many facets. It was the creation of the *rose cut* in the diamond, commonly twenty-four facets but sometimes thirty-six, that changed the style and character of jewelry by the early eighteenth century. The rose cut originated in the Netherlands but spread over Europe like a gossip vine. Silver was widely used as a mounting or setting for diamonds, as it was reasoned that it would complement the stone without competing with it.

Once Vincenzo Peruzzi invented the brilliant cut, however, every woman in the world seemed to have the urge to one day own a diamond that sparkled like the stars and held the colors of the rainbow in its bright rays. The diamond reached its maturity the day the talented Venetian produced his first brilliant cut of fifty-eight facets. Unlike the pearl, whose luminous gown is beautiful as it comes from its sea bed, the diamond needed to be coddled into its rare maximum beauty, and Peruzzi found the way.

The domed cabochon cut is never found in a diamond. To hide the diamond in such a bland cut would be like putting a heavy veil over a beautiful face. Diamonds must be faceted, and properly, to show their rainbow colors—a glorious treat to any eye.

Diamond cutters are a very special kind of lapidary. And as mentioned, while all other gem cutters are called "lapidaries," diamond cutters are known as just that, "diamond cutters." Entrust your diamonds to only these specialists. Diamond cutting has helped to make the diamond more precious. In antiquity the ruby and other stones took precedence over the diamond. The reason is apparent. Earlier diamonds were not faceted properly, the brilliant cut being unknown until Peruzzi introduced it early in the eighteenth century; the domed cut could not be used to advantage and other cuttings added little or no beauty to the gemstones and gave no hint of the dazzling rainbow hues possible.

A diamond cutter must use exquisite as well as precise judgment in handling a good diamond. Although the shallower Koh-i-noor may not be considered as beautiful by some as when it was 186 carats, we might mention that in spite of its beauty in its natural Indian form, *it did have four flaws in it*. That is apparently why Queen Victoria wanted it cut. The flaws *were* removed; and while it was reduced to 108 carats, the gem was finally pure. When you have a queen's treasure you can whittle away seventy-eight carats without flinching. And being a queen, Victoria cherished quality over quantity. I have seen two models of the Koh-i-noor Diamond in its Indian shape—one in the armlet in which it was presented to the Queen and the other alone, and in that form it looks lopsided—as though someone had sliced a piece from one side of it. To my mind it needed cutting and the particular artistry that was used to fashion it into its present form should be warmly applauded. It is far, far more symmetrical now. Not as heavy, perhaps, but incredibly more beautiful. Its fire and light are unforgettable.

As many rock hounds have proved, diamond mining in the United States can be as exciting as going to "Golconda," if it were possible to mine there now. It is interesting to note that the greatest mining engineers in Kimberley, the South African Mines, trained in the United States. The Colorado School of Mines is famous. All told, we've come a long way from the days when they rubbed two diamonds together to polish them.

A diamond wears well because of its unequaled hardness. If your husband or your man of the hour demurs buying one, just remind him it doesn't have to be turned in *every* year like his automobile. It won't wear out—ever. What beauty is not enhanced by the added beauty of diamonds—especially by candlelight? *You* could be that beauty, wearing diamonds you mined.

Although diamonds have been controlled so that they have never reached the market like a waterfall of peapods or rice, they have known some vulgar popularity. During the nineteenth century, a gentleman, apparently enraged by the sudden popular use of the diamond, said, "The diamond has become notoriously common since every tradesman has taken to wearing it on his little finger." When I was a child I had much the same idea. All the vulgar men I saw seemed to have a diamond ring, which is probably why I associated it for such a long time with a gaudy background. The diamonds that flashed in front of me were always on a hand, quite possibly holding a cigar—the price of which its owner had recounted many times—and the hand was invariably pudgy.

Bit by bit the *nouveau riche* man seems to have given up his diamond ring for a spectacular car. Somehow the recession of the diamond from male hands has made it a more valuable piece of jewelry to me—and, I am sure, to others. Now I look at it only for its beauty and the power it has to make any other stone that associates with it more beautiful. The diamond is *not* a man's stone, however. Somehow, he generally looks showy behind it. There is one exception. Napoleon wore the *smartest* diamond I have ever seen in the hilt of his sword. It looked like it belonged to a *man*, and to someone with great, good taste.

Since diamonds are frequently found by gold hunters, it is interesting to read a theory Plato had about the diamond. He saw the diamond as a kind of kernel formed in gold, and supposed it was the noblest and purest part of the metal that had been condensed into a transparent mass. In somewhat the same vein Jerome Cardan said in the sixteenth century, "Precious stones are engendered by juices that distill from precious minerals in the cavities of rocks. The diamond, the emerald, the opal from gold; the sapphire from silver; the carbuncle, the amethyst and the garnet from iron." No matter how technically inaccurate the old mineralogists were, they gave another bright dimension to the precious stone. I like to think of the diamond and the emerald as the juice of gold!

The same man turned philosopher when he said, "Precious stones have fewer flaws than animals and vegetables but because their brilliance sets them on view we notice the flaw. It is like a famous person. The luster of their fame renders their faults more apparent, while the ignorant and the vulgar, under the veil of their obscurity, escape having their vices noted." In the time of Jerome Cardan precious stones were considered living things and he treated them that way.

There are certain stones that require special handling to make them even more than they are and the diamond is one of those. If you set a diamond well—in its maximum setting —you will seem to have a stone of considerably larger size than it appeared unmounted.

I was discussing the diamond with a friend. "Ah," said I, "with your great head of knowledge you must know much of the gem world. Tell me about the diamond." He begged off as having a depressing sense of inadequacy about the gem kingdom and then proceeded to give me a gem of a quote.

"The only thing I have come across is quite useless. It was a remark by one of the Populist orators that 'the diamonds that bedecked the wives of the grain speculators were the frozen tears of the farmers' wives.' "

This is an age of exhibitionists, an age, it seems, when everyone wants to express himself—whether he has something important to say or not—and somehow that is not too bad. But I think we don't do the things we perform with class, with that flourish that makes one remember the moment with a lift. . . . Now, take the King of Saxony. He wore the Green Diamond, a gem of enormous size, *as a button to the plume of his hat*. I think it is the kind of thing today's pace-setters are reaching for, but they simply haven't achieved it with the same aura of style and class. And then there was Henry VIII. He had a collar of magnificent rubies. Of course someone appreciated them even in those days, because to my knowledge they aren't in the British royal regalia, and no one knows quite what happened to them. Cromwell had a nasty habit of doing away with the jewels of the kingdom so it might be that Henry's ruby collar went the way of Oliver Cromwell's whim —or whip.

Since diamonds of significant size and quantity have been found in at least fifteen counties in Georgia, one must assume they are there. We haven't done an entire chapter on gold, as that is quite another story and would make another book, but many of the diamonds in Georgia have been found where people were seeking gold. Dahlonega is a spot where you can pan and quite possibly find gold, and perhaps some other precious goodies. A friend from Long Island, New York, went to Dahlonega and afterward showed me the most beautiful gold crystal nugget you have ever seen, which he found there. You don't know what finding your own golden treasure is until you have seen a piece of glorious glittering crystallized gold—and *you* may find it at Dahlonega.

If you look for diamonds and happen to find a gold nugget the size of an orange or even the size of a gooseberry, you can't call it a lost day. But if you are the type who might throw back the gold—"take back your gooooold for goooooooold will never buy me," as the song goes—you will be interested to learn it has been reported through the Georgia Department of Mines, Mining, and Geology that diamonds have been found in the following places: White, Hall, Habersham, Lumpkin, Dawson, Banks, and Clayton counties. Most of these counties lie in the gold belt of the state, and the finds there have been the result of rather extensive panning operations. So, there is great danger of your finding gold if you don't find diamonds. No *source* rock has ever been found in Georgia, however. Perhaps we can tinker a bit with Plato's idea that the diamond was a kernel formed in gold or Cardan's lovely thought that diamonds are the juice of gold. The ancients had a way of making everything sound so interesting, you want it to be true.

There are diamonds in Indiana, but it seems they are usually found by someone panning for gold. Grains and flakes of gold have appeared in a number of counties in Indiana. Morgan County and Brown County have both produced gold *and* diamonds.

It is generally conceded that the gold found in almost two dozen counties in Indiana does not have a source rock in that state, but is the result of being transported by glaciers from points in the north or northeast and deposited as glacial debris. Since it is known that many of the moving masses of ice came down to Indiana during the glacial period, there is every reason to believe that both the gold and the diamonds found in that state are glacial deposits.

Indiana is a place where tiny garnets of various shades are found in company with the gold. Besides the two counties already mentioned Cass County, Clark County, Ohio, and Dearborn counties may have gold too. Franklin, Greene, Jefferson, Jennings, Morgan, Putnam, Montgomery, Warren, and Vanderburgh are also counties where you might find gold.

Since the incidence of finding diamonds while washing drift gold is very high in this state, there is a chance that you will find one or the other of these bits of treasure for your pains. The interesting thing about the diamonds taken from Brown and Morgan counties is their colored beauty—pink, blue, yellow, and a toasted-yellow shade. Add Indiana to your list of possible diamond find areas.

It has been said that where there are garnets there are almost always diamonds. A nice thought! An intriguing idea, as you will realize when you get to the chapter on garnets, is that there might be diamonds right in the heart of New York City. Don't scoff, the street railway people in Boston are reported to have found diamonds there.

Also, if you will look into the matter you will find that diamonds exist in Pike County, Arkansas, as we have said, but they have also been found in Wisconsin (the Theresa Diamond of 21.25 carats was found there in Washington County near Kohlsville); Virginia (the Dewey Diamond of 23.75 carats was found there); West Virginia (the Punch Jones Diamond of 34.46 carats turned up there); Minnesota, Michigan, Montana, Illinois, California, Ohio, Indiana, Alabama, Kentucky, Texas, Tennessee, Idaho, and in Cleveland County, North Carolina. South Carolina rumors some diamonds with gold.

It hasn't been the scarcity of diamonds in the world that has kept their price up and their demand constant, but rather the way the output of diamonds has been controlled and delicately exploited. The diamond is a forever stone, the most durable of gemstones, and its romantic dimensions have been well publicized through the ages. No self-respecting bride would allow herself even to consider the strains of *Lohengrin* until the man of her dreams had at least mentioned the word carat when he wasn't speaking of a vegetable.

It is a provocative treasure, this grease-coated, onion-gray, rough beauty, whose glorious face is generally revealed when proper polish and cutting are applied to it.

What a marvelous objective to have for your summer holiday—to find a diamond the size of a hen's egg. The sad thing is that you will let someone talk you out of it and you'll sit at some seaside resort, drinking charged water, staring into tomorrow, never thinking that some of the great stones in existence have been found on beaches—just like the one on which you are wool gathering, perhaps—where someone took the trouble to look.

11

❧

Green as Grass? It Could Be an Emerald!

Until I penetrated the world of emeralds I was probably one of the few gem collectors who had not been snared by the green garment of that elusive gemstone. I did not think the emerald was beautiful, and in spite of its rareness—as with chinchilla—I thought there was something dry and somewhat cold about it. Mostly I was put off by the cutting. The emeralds I saw were either cabochon or a bland emerald cut that seemed flat and lifeless. Actually I wasn't really *seeing* the gem. In those days I think I would have rejected emeralds as coat buttons, but now I challenge anyone to wave a package of the green goddesses before me and dare me to sew them on anything. The anything could be my face.

Emerald is a variety of the mineral beryl, the only precious variety. Like pure corundum, pure beryl is colorless. It is the chromium in it that colors it green. It is awesome to think of the rare and valuable emerald and realize that the difference between the beryl emerald and the considerably less valuable aquamarine is that minuscule trace of chromium that identifies it as a true emerald just as the aquamarine depends on traces of iron for *its* color.

When you are remembering the fine shade of difference in chemistry and the vast market value difference between aquamarine and emerald think of the aquamarine crystal found by a miner in 1910 in a pegmatite vein in Brazil. Its transparency was so perfect, it could be seen through from end to end. It measured nineteen inches in length and sixteen inches in diameter. It was sold for $25,000. Reflect, if you will, on what that stone, which looked like an old-fashioned block of ice, might have been worth if inclusions of chromium instead of iron were its oxide.

The word emerald comes from the Latin *smaragdus*. Aquamarine, of course, comes from the early descriptions of its relation to the sea with its marine colors. It was Pliny, the ancient mineralogist, who said that aquamarines are stones "which imitate the greenness of the clear sea."

There is another form of beryl that is semiprecious and prized besides aquamarine—the beautiful pink morganite. This delightful, blush-toned stone was named after John Pierpont Morgan, the financier and philanthropist. The pink shade of it is attributed to lithium. Heliodor, an outmoded name for yellow beryl, like aquamarine, is colored by traces of iron.

An emerald is not found in gravel. It occurs in the rock in which it is formed, and is always mined from the parent rock, which has been exposed through weathering, at the surface. In mining emeralds you might use picks or crowbars as tools. Emerald crystals are recovered by hand and cleaned with acid. Great care should be taken not to pick or chip out the gemstone too close to the matrix or stone that surrounds it. Sometimes when the emerald has surfaced through its white limestone matrix, much of it, like an iceberg, might be just under (or behind) the matrix at which one is chipping and a large, hidden part of the gemstone could be irreparably shattered. This is no small tragedy.

Because the emerald is almost invariably flawed, it has passed into proverb as unattainable perfection. A perfect emerald is one of the rarest of gems. "Like an emerald without a flaw" is an infrequent and pure compliment, similar to the ruby proverb. It has been said the most desirable shades of emerald are rare, and almost always flawed. Less than one percent of the emeralds found are of good quality. Like all weak things, pale emeralds—for all the wealth their stronger sister shade brings—are worth little.

The emerald has been around a long time. It was a great source of wealth to the ancient pharoahs, and it is said Cleopatra's mine is still being worked in Egypt. This mine in Upper Egypt was abandoned for many years and rediscovered in the nineteenth century. For some reason, perhaps politics, it was closed again and not opened until the turn of this century. The popularity of the emerald with the ancients may have grown out of the fact that, like the ruby, it is a beautiful gemstone even as it comes from its mineral home. The sapphire and diamond are not. Both these latter stones stupefy one with their beauty when they are properly cut and polished.

Many stones are temporarily and hopefully mistaken for the velvet green emerald. Green garnet, green corundum (the oriental emerald we talked about earlier), and green tourmaline are some of the stones which might puzzle you. The reliance on the Chelsea Color Filter to separate quickly the true emerald from most other green stones is no longer realistic. Once, since the emerald appeared red in this test while most other green stones remained green, the Chelsea Color Filter was considered a good way of separating emeralds from non-emeralds. Now, even synthetic emeralds appear red through the filter and some natural emeralds do not. There is no on-the-mining-spot test or any other *quick* test to tell an emerald.

The majority of emeralds are emerald cut to show the *color* beauty of the stone. When an emerald is faceted, sometimes thirty to fifty percent of the weight of the rough stone is lost. However, the brilliance and color music of a properly faceted emerald are indescribably beautiful. I asked D. M. V. Manson of the American Museum of Natural History in New York which of all the gemstones he fancied and his answer was quick and decisive—"The emerald." And why? "Its color." Since this is a man who is surrounded by such treasures (recently stolen but returned, I might add) as the 563.35 carat Star of India, the largest star sapphire on record; the 100.32 carat De Long Ruby, and the Midnight Star Sapphire of 116 $\frac{5}{64}$ carats, he has had many chances to be lured by other gemstones. His praise is high praise indeed.

People who love emeralds find them the most glorious of all stones and color is the invariable lure. Now that I am closer to this lovely stone I believe the emerald devotee finds depths in it that intrigue him, as the stone seems an unfathomable mystery, like a beguiling woman, perhaps. An emerald is a stone into which you look down and down—finding anything you wish.

Pliny, in an ancient comment, mentioned the unchanging beauty of the emerald in that neither sunshine, shade, nor artificial light had an effect on its appearance. Emerald seems to be an untiring stone. Perhaps the green, the verdant note of it, suggests a new spring or eternal hope. Emeralds have also always been considered stones which have a helpful effect on tired eyes. The gem cutters of antiquity kept an emerald close by to refresh their eyes and reduce the strain of doing their fine work of cutting. Today lapidaries still find this soothing effect from the stone.

Robert Crowningshield of the Gemological Institute of America mentioned to me that the Topkapi Museum in Turkey probably has the finest emeralds one could see. That set me to plucking away at an English friend who had just returned from Istanbul and that museum. He *had* seen the incredible emerald collection and said one emerald he saw in the rough weighed about seven pounds. In his shocked state he could only view it as a large "lump of green." Without direction, he said, he would not have believed it was an emerald. Most of the gems he saw were set in ceremonials or tiaras, but he did see a pair of "braces" studded with emeralds and rubies and a coffee service blazing with rubies and emeralds laced with diamonds. There were also dazzling jeweled boxes and sword hilts and solid gold candlesticks with precious stones as well. Rooms and rooms of gems exposed themselves to make one wonder if he were in Aladdin's cave. A little side note: the Moslems have nothing that represents the living—no graven images—within the museum. In the old Moorish style it is built around a series of courtyards, and for security reasons all the windows open onto the courts.

One feels there must be mountains of emeralds, figuratively speaking, hiding in Spain. The South American emerald mines have always uncovered gorgeous emeralds, the best in the world, and in the days of the Spanish conquest fortunes in emeralds flowed into Spain like rivers of treasure. One can only weep for the beautiful emeralds that were lost when Cortez was shipwrecked in the sixteenth century. He had five choice gems cut in unique shapes for his bride. Perhaps you may find some hints among them as to what you can do with your emeralds when you find them. One of the Cortez emeralds was made into a bell with a pearl for a tongue. Another was fashioned into a rose. A third was a captivating horn. There was one cut into the shape of a fish with gold eyes. The most exquisite of all the creations was the emerald made into the form of a cup with a foot of gold.

Long before I knew emeralds for the grass-lush real gems they are I *was* intrigued by one particular emerald. I learned somewhere that the Hapsburgs owned what was represented to me as a tiny, four-inch-high jug cut out of a single emerald. If you must milk your tea, thought I, what more charming way to pour than from an emerald spout. Somehow it reminded me of Tillie Lewis' diamonds at the breakfast table. (I wonder what Oliver Wendell Holmes *would* have thought of Tillie.) In any event, I tracked down the treasure and found it was a jar for ointment, created in the seventeenth century for the Hapsburgs by Dionysio Misaroni, a Milanese. The jar is now thought to belong to the Austrian government.

Emeralds do something that could change a man's wallet from being partly filled to "empty." It seems emeralds are very flattering to the body. When women find that to be a fact of life they are likely to turn their cosmetics in for a jar of precious beryl. After all, when its own beauty is saluted the first order of a jewel is to flatter the wearer. Very few jewels do that. Some jewels stand apart from the body that carries them as though borrowed for the occasion, and frequently they are.

The emerald does not escape the legend cycle and its symbolism too was important to the ancients. It was worn as an amulet against fascination as it was thought to hold back the powers of the evil eye. The legends about emeralds go back so far they have multiplied with the ages. The ancient Egyptians called it the Lovers Stone, as it was supposed to increase love. If a man gave his lady love something that rare and costly, she could only look at him with increased feeling. Emeralds are also supposed to restore peace to troubled souls. Trouble would seem to be easier to live with if there were a storehouse of emeralds to help erase frown lines.

I never understood one legend, that the sight of an emerald struck such terror into the viper and the cobra their eyes leaped out of their heads. However, it is a comforting thought that something scares *them* so you might want to take along a great headlight of an emerald to protect you on your next jungle invasion just in case the legend has substance.

Emeralds were also believed to help the wearer to forecast events, preserve him from any kind of accident, and to stimulate the mental powers of the wearer. Babinet had an interesting theory on the superstition of being helped supernaturally by precious stones. He believed the hope of cure in a given situation became part of the cure itself. "Where the mind," he said, "has an influence on the bodily system, the imaginary cause must produce a very real effect."

Theophrastus, who was a pupil of Aristotle, divides *all* stones, not only the sapphire as many ancients did, into male and female. Some of the early mineralogists not only believed that precious stones were living things, they also believed that they suffered illness, old age, and death.

Archie Jellen told me a tale, which sounds like a fable, about stumbling on unexpected emeralds. He had gone to Colombia in South America to locate some good emeralds. I might mention here that the best emeralds in the world are reputed to come from near the village of Muzo, about seventy-five miles from Bogotá in Colombia. The largest emerald ever found in Colombia was discovered recently in the Tres Cruces Mine. The stone, which weighs nearly three pounds, was valued at approximately $300,000. That valuation, which was a tentative one, may change, however.

In any event, while in Colombia, Archie Jellen ran across a man who was selling many articles. He noticed a box encrusted with what looked like green crystals among the man's wares. He bought the box for a handful of dollar bills and learned later it was encrusted with emeralds. The man who owned the box had used it for stamps and each time he ran across an emerald he would just glue it to the box as a decoration—or for want of some other place to put it. I have seen the box. It is wooden and primitive, and the design in emeralds is somewhat like a glittering border. The box is very valuable but not very attractive, although its present owner is so proud of it he would not think of turning the gems into one of his glorious jewel settings. This is a piece of gemology he views with pure sentiment.

I had learned long ago that the largest emerald is one of 1,383 carats and is the property of the Duke of Devonshire. It is in rough form, however, and when cut might run second in size to the 1,200 carat Patricia, which is in the Museum of Natural History in New York. I don't know where those calculations leave that large "lump of green" in Topkapi, or the recently found Colombian gemstone. I also learned at the Gemological Institute of America that possibly the finest cut emerald was thirty carats and once belonged to the Czar of Russia. It is now probably part of the Russian crown jewels at The Hermitage in Leningrad.

You won't be too surprised to find there are emeralds in Ireland, that green, green isle, in the Mourne Mountains. If you don't know those lovely Irish hills, here's a little melodic pause from the gem world to introduce you through a charming folk song about

The Mountains of Mourne!

Oh, Mary, this London's a wonderful sight
With people here working by day and by night
They don't grow pa-tay-tees, nor barley nor wheat
But there's kinds of them digging for gold in the street
At least when I asked them that's what I was told
So I just took a hand at the digging for gold
But for all that I found there sure I might as well be
Where the Mountains of Mourne sweep down to the sea.

You remember young Peter O'Laughlin, of course
Well, now, he's here at the head of the force
I met him today, I was crossing the strand
And he stopped the whole street with one wave of his hand.
And there we stood talking of days that were gone
While the whole population of London looked on
But for all his great powers he's wishful to be
Where the Mountains of Mourne sweep down to the sea.

There's beautiful gels here, hark, but never mind
With beautiful shapes nature never designed
And lovely complexions all roses and cream
But O'Laughlin remarked with regard to the same
That he thought those roses he'd venture to say
On your lips the color might all come away
So I'll wait for the wild rose that's waiting for me
Where the Mountains of Mourne sweep down to the sea.

Once when I was collecting treasures for a charity auction I was given what was represented to me as an emerald bracelet. A woman who cherished emeralds looked at it and passed it back to me quickly after putting it to her cheek. At the question on my face she said, "It is not an emerald. It is too warm." It seems emeralds—as with all crystalline materials—are cool against the skin in a way their imitation sisters are not. It may be one of the quick (but I do not think, infallible) ways of telling whether you have a gem or just green glass. . . . Always check further than temperature.

There are emeralds in North Carolina, although I have never mined any, but some friends of mine found one that was 2.8 carats. One of my friends found emeralds in North Carolina in the area between Highlands and Cashiers. The emeralds from that area came from a mine called Sheep Cliff. However, more emeralds are found in the area of Spruce Pine near Asheville, North Carolina, than in any other place. The LARGEST emerald was found in Cleveland County near Shelby, North Carolina. The same friends found emeralds in Georgia. They dry mined these because there were no streams to wash them down. Fortunately the emeralds were in white matrix and together with their brilliant personal hue were easier to spot than the earth-colored rough sapphire or the rough ruby, which jump out under the water treatment but not in the dry soil and gravel mixture.

Although some emeralds have been found in Georgia, there is other beryl there too, as some lovely aquamarine has come from that state. (Just out from La Grange in Georgia, there is rose quartz of unusual quality as well as some beautiful tourmaline. One of the rare specimens of asteriated rose quartz was found there by someone I know. He tells me there are large quantities of rose quartz in the entire area.) But, to return to beryl, aquamarine of unusual gem quality has been found in Troup County near La Grange. All of the stones are of a rich blue-green and stones as large as fifteen carats have been cut from some of the material. More than thirteen hundred pounds of gem material has been recovered from this area alone. Rabun City, Georgia, may have some beryl surprises too.

Another friend found aquamarine in with the rose quartz at the Hogg Mine near La Grange. One carried her own water up the hill to wherever she was picking with a small ax or a miner's pick. It is wise to wear goggles, she tells me, to keep the small bits of quartz or rocks from entering the eyes as one works. The rocks are sharp and ate holes in the best pair of work gloves my friend wore, in a short period of digging and picking. Handling most stones (especially quartz) will not give you pretty hands, so do see that you are well protected from cuts because of the sharp crystals and surrounding stones.

The Connecticut beryl hunters will find good areas in Fairfield, Middlesex, and Litchfield counties there. Haddam in Connecticut, incidentally, is a good place for aquamarine. In New Hampshire you might penetrate the counties of Cheshire, Sullivan, Merrimack, and Rockingham. Shelby, Cleveland County, Big Crabtree Mountain, Mitchell County, and Stony Point, Alexander County, in North Carolina are beryl areas. Maine is a gem state: Oxford County has very good aquamarine and Androscoggin County as well as Sagadahoc and Cumberland counties there and Stoneham are good beryl possibles. You may find beryl in South Carolina, Nevada, Massachusetts, Pennsylvania, California (San Diego County), Colorado, Alabama, South Dakota, Wyoming, or Idaho. In Canada, Renfrew County in Ontario has aquamarine. Also try Kearney, Ontario. Emerald hunting can be fun as well as a clue to many more treasures. The emerald is one of the stones whose brittle texture has kept it from engravings of any great number or kind, but there is said to be an emerald of the Middle Ages with an unforgettable etching: "The Soul Led Away by Pleasure." The title alone is a provocation to seek the stone in some ancient treasure trove.

If your eyes are open and you are in gem country, you are reasonably certain to find *some* treasure. Let us hope it is a beautiful, candy-bar-size emerald lurking in micha schist or granite, waiting for your quick eye or mine to discover it.

~~~~~~~~~~~~~

Although there are, by most experts'
standards, only four precious gemstones—emerald, diamond, ruby, and
sapphire—through the ages two other
gems have seesawed up and not-quite-
down in continuing favor, the opal and
the pearl. These two "jewels" have too
much history to be placed in the sec-
tion on semi-precious stones so they
will be included in the immediately
following category of additional precious gems. We hope these pages will
help you know there is more and ever
more treasure to be taken from the
gem world around us than you might
dream.

12

❧

A Word about Pearls!

Pearls are organic, formed through a living organism. They come to us through specific mollusks which secrete the pearl material to reduce irritation. A parasite's egg—usually the larvae of a marine worm—is the beginning of a natural pearl. The pearl oyster and the pearl mussel are the best sources of pearl gems. The true pearl oyster has the mile-long name of *Meleagrina margaritifera* and the pearl mussel is called *Unio margaritifera*.

The little oysters you will find surrounding the horse-radish sauce on your dish at dinner are unlikely to produce a pearl of great price, but don't let that keep you from looking for one. A house guest of ours found one a few summers ago in a plate of smoked oyster hors d'oeuvres I served.

The "orient" of the pearl is its shimmering cape, its iridescence. The pearl is the most ancient of all gems, old, and loved by men and women. Perhaps, then, because of its antiquity, it is fitting that the loveliest pearls still come from the Persian Gulf. But, we have them too, we have them too. Don't be fainthearted.

Almamoun, considered one of the most generous of all the caliphs of Bagdad, is said to have showered a thousand pearls of the largest size on the head of his bride. It all sounds more ghastly than openhanded, however, since the tiny head of the just-wed lady must have ached right through the honeymoon. But, if one must be pelted with treasure, I suppose the pearl is as happy a selection as any other gem.

In spite of Almamoun, large pearls are a rarity. If they remain too long in their mollusk home, they malform. These malshaped pearls become baroque pearls, making lovely necklaces and other jewelry. They were quite popular during the Renaissance, but some consider them slightly sick pearls, something like overripe fruit, grapes too long on the vine.

Since pearls are a living thing, time and carelessness take their toll of them. You are not likely to see too many lustrous pearls from antiquity although you may find some finely preserved specimens, but you *will* find many beautiful gemstones as lovely as when they lay against the creamy throat of an ancient queen.

Pearls are part of every century. They are always with us and appreciated. They are always in style. I know, however, that they do not at the moment compete with the diamond in value or as collateral, as I once tried to help someone offer a $30,000 necklace as collateral to cover a real estate situation. She could not get even a fraction of their worth in collateral value and since they were a family treasure she was finally persuaded they were worth more in her family vault than in the local market place.

There are many shades of pearl from snowy white to dark cream tones. My special pet is a pearl you can find with a little adventurous probing in the Bahamas. If pink is guaranteed to make a man propose, every little dear between these words and the Siberian border should get on the nearest conveyance to Nassau—the treasure trove of the pink pearl.

Those of you who are weary of hunting husbands, quail, bargains, or a new soufflé recipe will find pink pearl hunting in the Bahamas one of the most esoteric as well as lucrative hobbies you could approach. And—if you tire of pearls—you can always open the shell of the conch (pronounced "konk") and eat the delicious meat of this island shell fish that is the source of the pink pearl.

The conch is worth the hunt because while the pink conch pearl is not a deadly rival of the oyster pearl in value, a man who owns one of the finest collections of conch pearls in the

Bahamas says "they are worth from five to thirty dollars each, depending on size, shape, and color." I checked my strand of modest oyster pearls and discovered that, at the minimum pink conch pearl rates, they would be worth $250 and at the maximum $1,500. It's little check-outs like this that make you realize your pearl hunt *could* pay for your trip.

The pink pearl, which is oval or round in shape, is found in the lip of the conch. It ranges in shade from delicate ribbon pink to vibrant tones of flamingo. The darker the shade the more valuable the pearl.

When you consider that the natives find something like ten thousand conch a *day* (it is the staple dish of Bahamians) it is easy to understand how many pearls are overlooked because the fishermen concentrate on the conch as a food or for bait.

Up to fifty years ago, when it began to decline, pearl trading flourished in the Bahama Islands. Perhaps the "pearl hunters" will again revive the romance of hunting the pink pearl, and wouldn't you like to be part of *that* revival at thirty dollars a discovery.

The beautiful pink pearls can also be found in Florida in their native conch shells. And, while we are speaking of colored pearls, there are lovely blue and green pearls available from the abalone of California.

Cream-toned pearls may be found in Wisconsin, Oklahoma, Indiana, Arkansas, Iowa, Tennessee, and Illinois. The streams and rivers of this country have many treasures, and baskets of pearls are some of them. The pearls of precious value already found in the United States have been said to be the equal of the finest pearls of the Orient, whose pride in pearls is tremendous. Pearls are discriminating it seems because the best pearls come from mollusks in clean beds.

As with all gems, legend has followed the pearl, and if you are one of those people who forget to mail a letter or neglect an important birthday, grow close to the pearl—use it as your talisman—because the pearl is believed to strengthen a weak memory.

Fishing for pearls is one of the easier gem hunt activities. Night hunting in shallow waters produces many pounds of mollusks; crowfooting is another method of catching mussels, especially from river bottoms. Lines are attached to an iron bar and heavy wire is made into prongs like a bird's foot at the end of each line. This is dragged behind a boat scooping up the shell fish. Current techniques, however, consist of a diver who is lowered to the oyster beds, where he collects the mollusks in a wire basket and sends it up to be emptied by his boat companions as he seeks out fresh areas.

The pearl, briefly, is composed almost exclusively of lime and organic matter. The substance composing the pearl is identical to the iridescent lining—mother-of-pearl or nacre—of the shell.

Once the luster has gone from a pearl, only the most professional and tedious treatment may revive it. That is why care must be right and constant. You can't forget you have pearls. Losing them or breaking them isn't the only thing that can happen. Even the perspiration from one's body can affect them. They are a living thing, and if ever the theory of gems falling ill and finally dying had to be proved, it is demonstrated in the pearl. Pearls found in old tombs crumbled when they were touched much as the body turns to dust. Pearls are organic and demonstrate their relation to living things by behaving like their species. It is one of the few gems that is not durable and yet has maintained its popularity through the ages.

I had learned that if you cut a pearl you will find that each layer is like every other layer, because the structure has concentric shells. Hence, I was sure that if I mismanaged my pearls I could peel off one layer and get to the next with its iridescence intact. I found the technique is a delicate one, and unless the pearl is very valuable it is not worth pursuing. Protect them instead.

While it is lovely to have pearls with your gemstones when you set them, if you wish them for posterity or as heirlooms for your family remember the pearls may crumble long before the durable rubies and diamonds show even a dull film.

The unit of pearl weight is the pearl grain, which is a quarter of a carat. The seed pearls are sold by the carat. The spherical pearl is the most sought after.

The Mississippi Valley rivers produce some good fresh water pearls. The Gulf of California is another pearl treasury. Explore Rock River in Illinois and Wisconsin. Try the lakes and streams of Litchfield County, Connecticut and the streams of northern New York in Rockland County. Try Greenwood Lake, New Jersey, Middlesex County and Hampshire County in Massachusetts, the waters of western Maine. Try the Schuylkill near Tamaqua and Mahonoy City, Pennsylvania, the waters of Chesapeake Bay, Kent County, Maryland, the James and Powell Rivers, Virginia, and Tacoma Creek, Washington. Try the Wabash River, Indiana; Detroit River, Michigan; Ohio River, Ohio; Green and Tennessee rivers in Kentucky; Spring River, Kansas; Current River, Missouri; Alabama and Tennessee rivers in Alabama; Cooper River, South Carolina. Many streams in Ontario and Quebec have yielded pearls of fine quality.

Colored pearls, like colored diamonds, are beautiful and valued—but white, unblemished pearls are the most prized. Delicate blush shadings or creamy tinges can only enhance the pearl, however. Colored pearls may be pink, green or blue, as we have already said, but they may also be black, deep yellow, or bronze.

It is easy to feel guilty when one thinks of the bad handling she has given pearls in her lifetime. I had a pearl necklace of uncommon beauty, admired by everyone who saw it. I treated that strand of pearls with the same regard I have for hair pins and found they were not so hardy. Although my hairdresser pleaded with me not to put on my pearls before he sprayed my hair I thought his advice unwarranted and I had to save that second and a half besides. Suddenly I discovered that my pearls were, as the ancients would say, "sick," and later I found they were not going to get better. My amethyst clasp set in gold weathered the abuse, but the pearls, every other one, became gray, lost their luster, and now look like they had been dipped in lime juice. I can tell you those new pearls which arrived last Christmas have been cherished and pampered and cared for with unique attention. Prevention in the care of a gemstone is considerably easier than correction. I have read of ameythsts being destroyed or deteriorating when worn by someone accustomed to alcohol. It is easy to understand the chemical changes in the body under such circumstances and that a deleterious effect on a gemstone is just as likely as that one's finger might become blackened by gold jewelry when acid in the body is extreme.

Knotting pearls is a great help in keeping them longer and losing only one at a time if the string breaks through some accident. Pearls are strung now so that it is almost impossible to tell the knots are there, and still they are protected. I can think of nothing more beautiful than having a precious stone that you have mined yourself set in a clasp for a strand of pearls.

Pearls are beautiful, fragile gems that remind one they are "today" rather than "tomorrow" jewels, but I *have* seen fifteenth century pearls in Vienna that are still beautiful. One Austrian treasure I found enchanting was the Christening Set drenched in tiny pearls ordered by the Empress Maria Theresa. This particular one was white silver moiré with gold embroidery and what they considered "pearl trimmings." There was also a pillow on which the child was brought to the ceremony, and coverlets and baptismal robes achingly lovely still. Alive with tiny pearls, the small garments were very touching and in quite good condition.

I had been told there was a pearl of three hundred carats in the Imperial Crown of Austria. I saw the crown, which until 1804 was known as the Crown of Emperor Rudolph II, and a great pearl was there indeed. When I looked at it I was not thinking of pearls or precious stones specifically, but I do remember thinking how meticulously the symmetrically devised crown was. I stopped at the postcard booth and bought two copies of it in color because it represented such perfection in beauty. It is the masculine counterpart in beauty to the crown of the Queen Mother of England with its treasured Koh-i-noor and its delicately placed smaller diamonds. An interesting note about the Austrian crown is that no one has been crowned with it. For coronations the official Imperial Crown, also called the crown of the Holy Roman Empire, was used.

If you do not plan to go "pearling" and just want to stay with rubies, diamonds, sapphires, emeralds, or those little old semi-precious stones, why not put aside a squirrel bank account for yourself to pay for a strand of good cultured pearls and "clasp" it with your first mining finds? You cannot imagine the beautiful clasps that can be made from the most modest rubies and sapphires. If the strand is small, a single small stone set in a gold claw or some other frame will be beautiful. But remember, remember, the pearl is of animal origin and while so beautiful when fresh and alive, it can become very shabby and scruffy. This fragile gem does not hold up under time and neglect as the gemstone does.

Cultured pearls are grown by a mollusk, but instigated by man. The natural pearl needs no one to assist it, not even a lapidary. The natural pearl when it comes from its watery home wears its own shimmering beauty. This gem, which is the birthstone for June, is the jewel that is dedicated to Venus, and no wonder. This is beauty that cannot be made more beautiful, cannot be helped by the art of man—although man can *destroy* its beauty. Nature did her best to give us the pearl as a lovely, living thing. It is worth the "plunge" to find it anywhere.

Imagine the beauty a pearl diver sees at six to eight fathoms, which means thirty-six to forty-eight feet, the depth of oyster beds for best health and abundance. At that depth, corals and sponges and starfish are plentiful and provide a marine world of breathtaking beauty.

The precise formation of the pearl is not too often detailed, so the following might be helpful in getting to know specifically how it occurs. Most of the molluscous animals, which are aquatic and reside in shells, are provided with a fluid secretion with which they line their shells and give to the otherwise coarse material of which the shell is formed, an attractive, smooth surface which prevents any unpleasant friction upon the extremely tender body of the animal. This secretion is laid in thin, semi-transparent films, which, because of such an arrangement, have a striking iridescence and form in some species a sufficient thickness to be cut into useful and ornamental articles. The material in its hardened condition is called nacre by zoologists and is known commercially as mother-of-pearl.

Pearls, the pearly lining of the shells, detached and generally spherical or rounded portions of the nacre, are often found on opening the shells and undoubtedly these are the result of the intrusions of a parasite's egg, usually the larvae of a marine worm. This intrusion irritates the tender body of the animal, obliging it in self-defense to cover the cause which it has no power to remove. As the secretion goes on regularly to supply the growth and nacre of the shell, the included body gets its constant share and continues to increase in size until it becomes a pearl. Regular coatings of the nacreous secretion result in a gem.

If you are looking for something to collect that has many uses, you might seek out the pearl. And if you would set yourself an ambitious project, promise yourself a pearl *sautoir*. That is a strand of forty inches or more in length. With a long term project like that in mind, how can anyone think she has nothing to live for? Perhaps one day you'll stumble on some of the famous "ropes of Catherine," the de Medici who kept those treasures close to her until she passed them on to the willing beauty of Mary Queen of Scots, who lost them to another dozen queens.

13

❧

The Lucky or Unlucky Opal?

The opal has been in and out of the list of precious stones through the years, but when you consider the brilliant beauty of just one variety, the fire opal, as well as the better-known white iridescent species, then not recording the opal as a precious gem *is* an omission.

The word opal comes from the Latin *opalus* and the Sanskrit *upala*, meaning precious stone.

Opal is an amorphous mineral, one which is structureless—of indefinite shape. It is sometimes referred to as a mineraloid. Don't get gem opal mixed up with geyserite, which is a white or grayish shade of common opal. As the name would suggest, these form around the geysers and you might find them at Yellowstone National Park, Wyoming. Opal is frequently associated with volcanic rocks as well as being found in sediments and deposits from hot springs.

The opal never occurs in crystal form, except as a pseudomorph (that is, with the crystal form of another mineral) and it has no atomic structure in spite of its many appearances.

The color of opal depends on the way you see it. The rainbow hue grows out of the interference of light rays as they are reflected from extremely thin layers that consist of minute spherules of silica. These layers diffract light (in much the same way as the feathers of the hummingbird do, according to Dr. Ernest H. Rutland of the Geological Survey in London), and so give rise to the iridescent colors. The brilliant colors of almost every other stone—the garnet, the ruby, the emerald, the sapphire and the amethyst—are seen in the iridescent beauty of a fine opal.

The black opal is a dark opal and you might find it in Humboldt County, Nevada. Its background color is actually gray or deep blue, and the rainbow fires that leap from the gem are gorgeous. According to most authorities, the best black opals in the world come from Australia. The loveliest black opal I have ever viewed was from Lightning Ridge, New South Wales. The blues, greens, and reds that rose out of it like flying fish were mesmerizing. Blue was the predominant shade, and it was almost the color of lapis lazuli in its brightness. Virgin Valley, Nevada, has also produced some exceptional black opal.

Fire opal has a fiery red, red-gold, or orange sheen and background. White opal has multicolored flashes from a pale-colored background. Opal is colorless when pure, but nearly always milky and opaque or tinted dull shades by ferric oxide, magnesia or alumina. I have seen what is called "cherry opal" from Mexico, which is not cherry at all, but is rather orange like a sunburst.

Opal is one of the gems that may lose its moisture after it is mined. Its delicacy has been much discussed: some say opals can be protected by sealing them in glass jars, keeping them cool or moist, dipping them in alcohol or lacquering them. Since opal is regarded as a thirsty gem it has also been suggested that it be dropped in water occasionally. I have read, too, that an opal might be maintained by keeping it in a raw potato. However, since a stable opal need not lose water and since immersion in water has damaged some opals, the best care for this gemstone would seem to be not to expose it to sudden temperature changes . . . a major weakness of the stone. Because it is so brittle and sensitive to heat, maintaining an opal is not the easiest thing to do.

Opal is so delicate-looking, even as an uncut stone, that it is a bit difficult to believe that it is really solidified jelly. Of such a stone one expects the myth that it might be the baby teeth of a fairy queen thrown over her left shoulder long ago only to spring up into a world of iridescent gems. The Romans held the opal in such great esteem that one Roman senator preferred death to giving up his opal ring to Nero.

Opal is similar to quartz and might be confused with it except that it is softer. It requires great care in setting too, so that it will be protected adequately from jolts and scratches. Its hardness runs between 5.5 and 6.5. When you come upon an opal you might confuse it with quartz, so remember it can be scratched by quartz, which means opal is *softer*. Opal can scratch glass, however.

The fire opal is often faceted, but usually opal is cut *en cabochon*. Because it is fragile, generally small, porous, and easily spoiled, it requires great care and judgment in handling.

The opal enjoys strange popularity levels. It is loved or hated, sought out or feared. The supersitition that you must never wear an opal if it is not your birthstone is observed by many people. While the opal might not enjoy the greatest popularity as a gem to wear, the black opal is considered very rare, and brings a fine price.

Although the legend of being an unlucky stone is attached to the opal, its advocates say it possesses all the merits of the gems whose colors are seen in its iridescent beauty. That would seem to be more good luck than any one stone could possibly carry when you remember its flashes of ruby, sapphire, emerald, garnet and amethyst. The black opal is deemed by people who own one to be a gem of great GOOD luck.

There is much charm attached to the stone itself. The opal which might be white or pearl-gray, when held between the eye and light becomes pale red or wine-yellow with a milky transparency. By reflected light the colors of opal are vivid and of memorable iridescence.

When the color of the opal is arranged in small spangles it is called harlequin opal. Sometimes it exhibits only one of its colors. Most esteemed are emerald-green or orange-yellow, called golden opal. The opal exhibiting all colors with red predominant is the most costly and revered. That was probably what Pliny was speaking of when he likened the shade in an opal to the "burning fire of the carbuncle." Hungarian opals were sometimes referred to as Oriental opals because they were carried to the Orient and then shipped to Europe.

There are several places in Oregon where the opal might be found. Malheur, Morrow and Klamath counties are definitely recommended by the State Department of Geology in Portland, Oregon. When you learn to recognize opal you might find it in California—try San Bernardino County and Kern County there—also Emmett in Gem County, Idaho or Idaho City, Idaho. Idaho and California are two states that have volcanic rocks. You might stumble onto some of the colorless variety of opal in North Carolina in pegmatites in the Spruce Pine area. There is opal in Yuma County, Arizona, too; also Gallatin County, Montana, and Corson and Campbell counties in South Dakota.

Fire opal can be found in Mexico. And since it is such a gala holiday spot you might, in your first gem hunt, combine the satisfying pursuit of one of the loveliest of gems with a vacation in another country very close to home. It has been said the best species of fire opal is formed at Queretaro, but Esperanza and Zimapan in the State of Hidalgo in Mexico have produced glorious specimens. Decomposed trachyte is the parent rock.

Two Americans who left Florida ten years ago for a vacation in Australia are still there following the lure of the opal. They own what has been called the largest cut opal in existence. Weighing 34 ounces, it is 5,232 carats and has been named Darlene's Fancy after one of the owners. Don Heath and his wife mine, buy, sell and cut opals. They sold an opal almost the size of a loaf of bread to a fellow American. Considering that top-grade rough opal which sold for $6 an ounce in 1933 now sells for $1,000 an ounce, the Heaths are a pair of very lucky opal hunters indeed. Their home and shop as well as their mining activity is all done on Coober Pedy, where they live underground. Since the dust there blows from every direction all day long, and the region has constant raging winds combined with freezing winter temperatures and 140-degree heat in summer, living below the ground is a practical—if esoteric—way of life for this particular pair of gem hunters.

Precious opal in a geode is quite a sight. I saw one in the smallest geode I have ever viewed. The geode could not have been more than two and a half inches wide. Opal that has been colored green by nickel oxide looks like pale jade in its rough form. I have seen colorless opal that looks like crackle glass. The orange eye of fire opal looks like orange rock candy —and fire opal can be overwhelming. I have also seen it in deep, almost ruby-red, Chinese-red, bright orange, tangerine tinged, yellow, and gold. Whether brilliantly or cabochon cut, it is always a feast to the eyes. When you come upon a particular shade of common opal after seeing a fire opal or one of the more beautiful iridescent opals, you wonder how they could be of the same species or have the same name alliance at all. The common opal I most dislike is a tan, sandy beige, devoid of any color message. Its tones are as neutral as Switzerland.

Working on opal, since it is so delicate, would seem to involve the patience of Griselda wedded to the talent of Michelangelo, and I have seen some opal cameos that were, you won't be surprised to learn, in a museum.

One of my friends, a doctor who makes every moment of life count, is a rock hound; and he has some of the loveliest gemstones I have seen. Besides a breathtaking piece of lapis lazuli, nothing in his collection is more eye-compelling than his opals. This collection houses opals in almost every formation situation and in an incredible number of shades. He showed me a piece of what looked like smoothed out sea shell and as I looked down into its center, there, staring up at me, was one of the most beautiful fire opals I ever hope to see. He called it a petrified and opalized sea shell. I called it "gorgeous."

There was a piece of Mexican opal that was predominantly blue, and it looked like solidified satin—like a silken robe captured in motion—it was so fluid. One piece of rhyolite matrix (the rock in which the opal was embedded) held two different kinds of opal—one was the deep orange face of "cherry opal" and the other was a startling fire opal that none of us could take our eyes from. I have never come so close to being literally "fascinated." There were some lovely delights in his cabinets as well. He had two tiny turtles carved in their matrix studded with the opals still embedded in the rock as they were found. The rhyolite matrix wasn't particularly exciting, but the opal fires jumped from all parts to make the little figures an enchantment to the eye. There was also a fire opal fish carved in its matrix. Looking at these stones not only told me how many gemstones can be found if one looks for them, but also what charming ideas they generate as jewelry or ornament patterns.

Another friend told me the story of her personal hunt for opals. The gems were found in Twiggs County, Georgia. She said she found them in what is called the "overburden" of earth over the kaolin mines. "The boulders were opened by using heavy sledgehammers and wedges and a tool that looked like a chisel. Finally when the boulder was split—pried open between layers of crust and agate—there was a thin, narrow line of opal that resembled milk glass running horizontally. It was so hard to work with, we used it as a specimen rather than trying to peel it from the formations."

As with many mining expeditions, lovely things show up by accident. My friend continued her story of the opal quest. "After it became difficult even for the men to use the sledgehammer, the ladies started looking down the winding dirt road for sea shells. [All of this area had been underwater as part of the sea at one time and is called the Fall Line.] We found agatized trilobites—they looked like the corkscrew animals—shark's teeth, some agatized sand dollars, and a few river washed pebbles that looked like moonstones."

At another mine she received a box of the chalky earth with rocks and pebbles which she washed and sifted to find she had a lovely moonstone and a white opal, which Archie Jellen set after remarking on what a fine stone it was.

Here are some places where opal might also be lurking: Graham, Greenlee, and Maricopa, Arizona; Imperial, Inyo, and Mendocino, California; Nevada, California, as well as Sacramento, California. There is moss opal at Park, Colorado. Litchfield, Connecticut, and Washington, Georgia, have opal. Wallace, Kansas, has some. Jefferson and Wasco, Oregon, have it too. You may find some fire opal in Brewster, Texas. And there is opal in Presidio, Texas.

I had heard that Hungary was the chief source of precious opal until the Australian finds were made and I found Hungarian opal very lovely indeed. I viewed a shower of Hungarian opal jewelry at the Kunsthistorisches Museum in Vienna. The opals were interspersed with rubies and emeralds that were made into bracelets, a necklace, ear pendants, head pins, and a belt that were a gift from the city of Budapest to Princess Stephanie on the occasion of her marriage to Crown Prince Rudolph in the nineteenth century. Rudolph is the cutup who expired at Mayerling with his friend Marie Vetsera, under circumstances the Austrians are now reviving as "political." But anyone who has wept through the various remakes of the Mayerling tragedy prefers to think Rudolph "done himself in" for love.

On such a note I leave you to the opal—to discover whether it will be your lucky or unlucky gemstone.

~~~~~~~~~~~~~~

Moving among the magic of the multi-hued so-called semi-precious stones one is stricken that she can give only a nod to so many of the dazzling flower crystals the earth has yielded through the centuries.

There is room here to explore only the amethyst, the topaz, jade, and the garnet—with perhaps just a word or fifty about some other popular gem-stones.

14

❧

Garnets in a New York Park!

It is true that gemstones of one kind or another are found in all fifty states. Almost everyone holds to the creed that emeralds, diamonds, rubies, and sapphires are definitely precious gems—with opals and pearls always nudging the precious gem category for recognition. There are, however, many staggeringly attractive semi-precious stones, and one of the most elegant and rich-lustered of these is the garnet. Long ago when its meaning as a semi-precious stone was misty to me I chipped garnets from rocks in a park in New York City. I am sure the rocks are still there, together with other garnet-bearing stones. The spot is in Van Cortlandt Park, only a subway ride from mid-town Manhattan.

I have been told that garnets, oddly, have been found in the same areas as diamonds so it just might be that this time next year all 1,146 acres of Van Cortlandt Park will be torn up from one end to the other in the eternal quest for the precious diamond.

Don't fret if you don't find diamonds in the park—or even a bagful of garnets as I did. There's a consolation prize close by in the form of a lovely old eighteenth century house with a treasure in Early American antiques. I recently came across some of the garnets I chipped in that park, but after my finds in North Carolina, I must say, they looked very minor to me.

I remember our garnet hunting expedition well, and I recently unearthed a few snapshots of it. A few of us, fresh from the geology class of one of us at Columbia University, went with our little picks—an ice pick will do—to Van Cortlandt Park one Saturday afternoon to see if all the things written about the garnet were true. I don't remember how my friends learned the gems were there—probably a hint from the professor—but we went toward the shoulder-high rocks like homing pigeons. Soon we were chipping the stones with great speed as they were abundant, but quite small. Of course, *now* I think any stone that is not the size of one's thumb is minuscule—but in those days each stone we dug from the rock seemed a bit of treasure.

Like the ruby and spinel, the garnet was formerly called carbunculus or carbuncle, and we might presume it could have been in the ark with Noah too. Pliny called the garnet "carbuncle" from *carbo*, a live coal, because of its bright color. Garnet comes from the Latin *granatus*, meaning grain.

George Downing, who led our ruby safari, found some great garnets at Whiteside Mountain in North Carolina. He believes the best garnets are at Wildcat Ridge there. Garnets occur in several localities in Macon County, including a marvelous rhodolite garnet deposit located near the summit of Mason's Mountain on its southern slope, two miles west-southwest of West's Mills and one mile south of Cowee Creek, according to the North Carolina Department of Conservation and Development. Almandite, the commonest form of garnet, occurs in southeastern Macon County on the road to Whiteside Mountain, at the Macon-Jackson County line and also in a region two miles southwest of Dry Falls.

When one considers the great beauty of garnets, it is a bit depressing to realize that only a small amount of them are used as gem material. The largest percentage of garnets found is used for garnet paper or other abrasives. Gems, oddly, are the by-product.

Pyrope is considered a very good form of the garnet species, a magnesium-aluminum garnet, and makes a rich and colorful gem. It is a deep blood-red shade. Pebbles of pyrope have been found in the anthills of the Navajo Reservation in Arizona, so don't be too sure where you will slide on a slippery gemstone.

I have seen African garnets that looked like a large egg, but they are for collectors only, it seems. Smaller pieces I have seen were in a rainbow of colors.

Probably the most beautiful of the garnet species is the rhodolite garnet, an exceedingly rare stone compared to the abundance of the other varieties. Its color is said to resemble the tints of the rosy rhododendron. The rhodolite garnet can be found in gravel beds in North Carolina in the Cowee Valley area or Macon County and my friends have some wonderful specimens to prove it. Try the Mason Mine there. It is about five miles out from Gibson's and Holbrook's. There are small garnets, not rhodolite, at Holbrook's and Gibson's. The Mason mining was dry. My friends washed their stones in the stream. Of the rhodolite garnets they found, one was 4.5 carats and another was 5.4 carats. They were both polished into step or emerald cuttings. This cutting was used because it displays the color of the gem rather than its brilliance, and the rhodolite garnet, a beautiful rose pink, is the peacock of the garnet species.

There are so many varieties of garnet, many people, even though the stones are semi-precious, collect them to the exclusion of everything else. The very large collection of one garnet hound is now in the possession of the Museum of Natural History in New York. The stones are a dazzling sight, and there is no admission fee to view them when the gem collection is open.

The garnet, like all gems, precious or semi-precious, lives in legend and lore. It is considered the stone of constancy, is the birthstone for January, and is the talisman for travel. Once the garnet was used as an amulet to protect one from bad or horrendous dreams. But the most provocative thing I know about a garnet is that it was alleged, by the ancients, to lose its brilliance at the approach of danger.

Well, that is at least one good reason for trying to find a

garnet or *pietra della vedovanza* (stone of widowhood), as the Italians called it. This was because widows wore, and perhaps still do, garnet beads and pins ornamented with garnets. It is interesting that garnets, like amethysts, were considered a "right" stone for mourning—perhaps because both stones have a special elegance and dignity that neither lures you nor drives you away.

If you know someone whom you would like to impress, the symbolism of the garnet might intrigue you. It is supposed to promote sincerity. It is also a symbol of loyalty and devotion. Like many in that category of "semi-precious," such as cat's-eye and jadeite, which bring very high prices, that term is not particularly apt, and the garnet has fans who will never fail to cheer, buy, and wear it.

Albert the Great thought the garnet worthier than the ruby or red spinel, but gem experts today would disagree with him. However, this mineral of metamorphic rock has many admirers and the garnet would have more applause if potential fans could view the additional shades of light orange, crystal green, black, iridescent green, and burnt orange as well as the popular wine red, not to mention the rosy hue of the rhodolite.

The garnet has been around a long time, not only coming to us in delightful lore as the carbuncle, but it was frequently employed in jewelry and other ornatments during Egypt's Middle Kingdom, which is a lot farther back than yesterday.

Some believe the green garnet alone among colored gem stones has a luster approaching the diamond. It is understandable then that garnets have so often been mistaken for stones of superior value. One lovely, seventeenth-century necklace I saw in Austria was silver gilt with green garnets laced with pearls and red garnets. It was exquisitely delicate.

The Cape ruby, commonly quite ruby-red in appearance, refers to the pyropes and has often been called the Arizona ruby. If someone mentions Bohemian ruby to you do look knowledgeable, as it is a garnet, not a ruby. Of course you can look even more knowledgeable if someone mentions the ruby-tiger. That's neither a ruby nor a tiger—it's a moth.

Georgia is a state that has just about every kind of garnet—the whole garnet family, including a lovely blush-hued rhodolite. There you will find the blood-red pyrope, the reddish-brown and fiery red almandite, yellow-brown spessartite, and the grossularite in an opaque to red.

There are garnets in Oregon in Umatilla, Curry, and Josephine counties. The beautiful rhodolite garnet has been found in small crystals in a metamorphic rock near Woody's Gap in northeast Georgia. Almandite garnets have been found near Hiram, Paulding county, Georgia. Garnets come from Gila, Greenlee, Navajo, and Yuma, Arizona (Apache County there is sprinkled with garnets); Imperial, Inyo, Riverside, San Benito in California; Ruby Mountain and El Paso, Colorado; New London and Litchfield in Connecticut. Rabun County in Georgia is another spot for garnets; Benewah and Nez Perce in Idaho; Cumberland and Androscoggin, Maine; Baltimore, Maryland; Houghton, Michigan; Morrison, Minnesota; Lewis and Clark, Madison, Park, and Silver Bow, Montana; Washoe, Nevada; Cheshire and Merrimack counties in New Hampshire.

Sussex, New Jersey; Westchester, New York; Ashe, Macon, and Mitchell counties in North Carolina; Berks County, Chester, Delaware; Lebanon in Pennsylvania; Custer and Pennington in South Dakota. The Rutherford Mines in Amelia County, Virginia, are famous for garnet. If you think a New York park is not chic enough to hunt garnets you might try Alaska—southeastern Alaska. Or, nearer to home, a friend of mine found garnets on the beach at Lake Champlain near Plattsburgh, New York. Quebec has some garnets if you are lucky in your dig at Hull in Gatineau County there.

In dealing with gems, as with almost anything else, a little knowledge is a dangerous thing. We learn a few indisputable facts about mining and stones and consider ourselves experts much too early. It is very wise in the early stages of your mining hobby to put yourself in the hands of the professional gemologist or lapidary, who will guide and instruct you to the point where you can trust your own feelings about what is a worthwhile stone and what needs to be interpreted for you. You must see stones to know them. Words help a little, pictures a little more. But you must KNOW the rough stone. The experts themselves have been wrong so many times it behooves you to learn as much as you can about the stones you are interested in. If you trace the background of some of the largest gem finds in history you will realize that it took the instincts of one man, perhaps, to think he had a gem of great worth, but it was the trained eye or the instructed mind of many other people that corroborated that he indeed had a treasure. The Tuscany Yellow, the Arkansas Diamond sometimes called the Searcy Diamond, and many others went unsung until the right eyes and tests pronounced them first class gemstones, or conversely, as with the Black Prince's Ruby and the Braganza, realized that the one is actually red spinel and the other, perhaps white topaz—and not a diamond. This latter stone is in the Portuguese regalia and weighs 1,680 carats.

I have seen a four-rayed star garnet (en cabochon cut, of course) from Idaho that was not too beguiling alongside the dazzling beauty of a star ruby. It was the almandite garnet—purple tinged with red—but it looked so dark in the bad light in which I saw it that it resembled a gun-metal shade.

One delightful garnet I saw once was so large it was made into a covered dish. Although I saw the finished "gem" in Europe, the garnet came from a mine in the United States and I think it might have been from the Rutherford Mines in Amelia County, Virginia.

If you can live with a long name there is a hydrogrossular garnet, sometimes incorrectly called African jade. Some have bands of pink and green and remind one of watermelon tourmaline.

Small garnets are often rose cut. The garnet is, besides, a

stone that takes a wonderful polish. The relatively low degree of hardness makes it a good stone for engraving. A great art piece, "Sirius," was engraved on the well-known Marlborough garnet.

It seems to be time to revive the garnet, whose complexion is so elegant, whose fashion face is so timelessly lovely. It is time to make the garnet the fashion jewel it deserves to be, in or out of any century. Somehow, it belongs more to fashion than to preciousness, unless you unearth some of the gorgeous rhodolite, in which case you have fashion, beauty, and market value in a single gem. Tanzania produces the only commercial rhodolite at present.

15

✢

Amethysts You Can So Walk Upon

Although they are semi-precious and of the quartz family, which is a prolific one, amethysts have a born-to-the-purple look that even an emerald may not hold, it seems. Prized as a gem from ancient times, in spite of its current, un-chic abundance, many amateur collectors favor these lovely twilight-colored stones over all others. I wear one constantly and it dresses up a cluster of baby rings on my smallest finger into a conversation piece of daily rhythms.

Amethyst is the most valuable variety of quartz. Amethysts run in veins. They can run quite close to the surface or considerably below—a few inches or several feet from the earth's surface. The Blue Valley in North Carolina is a good spot to investigate. This is just out from Highlands, about eight or ten miles. There are gorgeous shades of rose amethyst as well as the prized purple shade there. This is approximately the spot where my small friend walked on the twilight gem (Macon and Jackson counties).

One friend mined amethysts and said the veins ran horizontally, like a trolley. You can dig to it and then pick it out. Away from the mines I have seen many amethysts as geode linings. These are mineral shells, about the size of a large grapefruit, with liners of amethysts (or other crystals or minerals).

In the same area, the same mineral situation, in which you find amethyst you are likely to find what has been represented to me as "smoky topaz." I believe it is smoky quartz. The best shade of amethyst is the pure, deep purple. It has been said amethyst, when perfect, resembles the violet or purple grape. You can find some glorious purple amethyst in Rabun City, Georgia. Besides North Carolina and Georgia there are generous quantities of amethyst in Montana, New Hampshire, Chester County, Pennsylvania, and also Virginia, Maine, Texas, Colorado, Arizona, and other states we will discuss in more detail later.

Unlike the emerald, the ruby, and the sapphire, no one is particularly anxious to pin-point or account definitely for what produces the color in the amethyst. It is very similar to rock crystal but for its beautiful shadings, which go from almost a lilac to violets of exquisite hue and very deep purple. It has been suggested this color may be due to manganese.

To leap into legend again—Albert the Great comments on its name, which in Greek, *amethystos*, means "not drunken," and offers that the amethyst is alleged to "counteract drunkenness, keeps one awake at night [I'm not sure I understand the positive blessings of that aspect of the gem], represses evil thoughts and confers a good understanding of what is knowable."

Just adhering to the possibilities of drama in gems should make any of us want to be bejeweled from the glimmer of one dawn to the next to reap the harvest of some of the legends. Incongruously, this gem is supposed to have been the gem of Bacchus, odd as that grape tale may sound—since the name means "not drunken." Bacchus, as one knows from somewhat revelous memory, was one of the thirstier Roman gods. However, association of Bacchus with the stone has nothing to do with actual thirst. It seems Bacchus in a fit of rage decreed that the first person who crossed his path would be eaten by tigers. (Is that what they mean by "don't cross him"?) Amethyst, a maiden on her way to worship at the shrine of Diana, was the victim. To save her, Diana turned her into a rock crystal figure. Bacchus, seeing the lovely quartz maiden, repented and, pouring wine over her, turned the beautiful figure into the present shade we know as amethyst. Pliny, incidentally, did not believe that wine and the lovely violet-hued stone had any connection.

Amethysts are a glorious fashion accessory because they add to almost any costume and go with almost any kind of day or evening wear. While the best amethysts are the deep purple shades, according to any expert, they must also be uniform in color throughout. One of the most important accessories of a gem collector is a magnifying glass. The greater the magnification the easier it will be to see the many extra flaws or beauties of one's gemstones.

Although a few locations have been suggested where amethysts might be found quite definitely, they, being of the quartz and commonest mineral group, might be found almost anywhere. Quartz forms under innumerable conditions and in all kinds of rocks. While you are looking for amethyst you might chance upon some of the pastel-bearing rose quartz. This is a stone that is frequently asteriated, and while it might not have the intrinsic value of the amethyst it competes against, you will have an ornament of great beauty if one of these falls into your line of vision or nudges your spade.

If one is a man of the grape, however, there is an ancient tradition that a man who drinks wine out of a vessel made of amethyst might drink all its contents without noticeable effect. It was also supposed to cure one of gout. But the most provocative promise of the amethyst as an amulet is that the wearer of the stone would become gentle and amiable through its influence as it preserved him from tempers and other outbursts. I wonder why no one ever brought the amethyst to Socrates' attention—it might have sweetened up his old scold wife, Xantippe. It was because of its many influences that the ecclesiastics wore amethyst as their bishopric jewelry, as it was understood to be good not only for the churchman who wore the amethyst ring but for the person who kissed it.

There is a snare involved in finding a first class amethyst. It might have good color in one part of the stone but not in another. When it does have richness, clearness, and uniformity of hue it is a gem of rare beauty. It comes in large stones so frequently that it can assign itself to almost any kind of ornamentation and can be used in limitless ways. As mentioned in the chapter on garnets, the amethyst is the only other stone that is worn with mourning.

It responds to an emerald or step cut. When associated with diamonds it produces a spectacular effect.

The ubiquitous Doradelle found one lovely deep purple amethyst crystal in the Hogg Mine near La Grange, where she was mining for rose quartz and aquamarine. Although George Downing found his amethyst in horizontal veins, Doradelle came upon hers in perpendicular or vertical formations. These she found in North Carolina. The quartz near the surface of the earth is called sugar quartz, and the further down she dug the better grade she found. Amethysts were also found not too deeply around the shallow roots of trees. She found her best smoky quartz in an area of this description.

"The amethysts I found in North Carolina were found with a guide who led my husband and a party of three others into some very lovely areas out from Highlands. We did dry mining, carrying mining picks and small, short-handled shovels. We were in a clay and sand area of a road bank. We would get on our knees, balance and dig in the earth. If we did not find any quartz crystals after going for several inches we would move into another area. After we found a few stones we would walk to the stream at the level below us, fetch the buckets, and wash the stones to see if they had color. Most of them cut into nice, light pink amethysts.

"The two crystals twinned together in the Hogg Mine were deep purple. We had them cut into nice small stones."

Few stones, precious or semi-precious, lend themselves to so many delightful ornaments as the amethyst. It is a stone that always seems to sit "above the salt." It isn't what could be called a quiet stone, but its elegance is such that it seems to find the right people rather than someone being lured by *its* lights. I feel the amethyst chooses its owners rather than the other way round.

Turning my back on the legend that the wearer of the stone BECOMES gentle and amiable through its influence, I think it chooses only soft, special people to wear its purple beauty. It makes a delicious promise to insomniacs, or anyone—if placed under one's pillow the amethyst promises sweet dreams.

This stone, whose name derived from the lyrical Greek, *amethystos*, has a beautiful alliance with gold when used in jewelry. I think very surely that being "born to the purple" must have some ties with being born to wear amethysts.

If you think the opening chapters of this book were a dream sequence hear ye, hear ye. Pale amethysts are found as lining vugs (openings) in a vein near Buckhead, a few miles from Madison, Georgia. As Professor James G. Lester, Chairman of the Department of Geology at Emory University tells it: "The vein crosses a gravel road and was exposed during grading, with the result that THE ROAD IS LITERALLY PAVED WITH AMETHYST CRYSTALS." I knew if I dug deeply enough I would find somebody else who had walked on amethysts besides my friends, the Downing family.

One of the most beautiful amethysts, according to Professor Lester, that was ever found in North America was discovered at Charlie's Creek, near Hiawassee, by Mr. Gilbert Withers of Atlanta. It is a deep purple with red reflections. A large display brilliant of seventy-five carats was cut from it and it is now in the Museum of the Georgia State Capitol.

Clarke County in Georgia is an area just being explored—and with great promise—for amethyst. Gila, Maricopa, Chochise, Greenlee, in Arizona have amethyst too. Colorado is a gem heavy state and you'll find amethyst in the counties of Mesa, Mineral, Saguache, and Teller. There's amethyst in Hartford, Connecticut, and in New Haven (and you thought it had only Yale!). Check Morgan County, Georgia; Oxford

County, Maine; Hampden and Hampshire, Massachusetts; Crawford, Missouri; Jefferson, Park, and Silver Bow, Montana; Clark, Nevada; Carroll, Cheshire, and Coos, New Hampshire; Passaic, New Jersey; Burke and Warren counties in North Carolina; Wasco, Oregon; Brewster, Gillespie, Llano, Jeff Davis and Presidio, Texas; Prince Edward, Virginia; Greenwood County, South Carolina. In Canada you might find some amethyst in Thunder Bay County, Ontario. Minas Basin and the Bay of Fundy should produce some if you get as far as Nova Scotia, which is noted for lovely quartz. My own most colorful experience with amethysts happened in London at the British Museum of Natural History. Everyone associated with the mineral collection at the museum had been most kind in giving his time and information about any stone I inquired after. One charming young man said, "I think you might be interested in the 'Blasted Amethyst.'" The name was so provocative I could hardly wait to hear its story.

"It's accursed," I was told. "It is said if you view it you will have bad luck." My interest waned in seconds as there is more than a tinge of superstition in my make-up, but the young man would not be put off. "I'll see if I can find it for you. It is locked away."

"It's too much trouble," I protested, visualizing my teeth falling out or my ear dropping down two notches as soon as I beheld it.

"No trouble at all," I was told, as he hunted a good five minutes from strong box to strong box until it was found.

"I'll look at the history you said was enclosed with it," I compromised. "That's really all I need for my story," I giggled nervously. He laid the Blasted Amethyst (that's what they call it at the museum) alongside the sheet of paper on which the history of its accursedness is chronicled. As I read the horrendous story I was less and less inclined to look at the gemstone, but the description was so provocative I began to cast side-long glances at the troublesome piece of jewelry. All

I can remember is that the scarabs were quite unlovely and whatever else was there, I was afraid of. However, so that you may at least share its promise of terror Dr. A. A. Moss, Keeper of Minerals at the museum, had a photocopy made of the Heron-Allen letter, containing the background of the gem, and gave it to me in London. He has graciously consented to have the letter reprinted here.

Copy of a letter written by Edward Heron-Allen (1861–1943) accompanying an amethyst * (also known as the Delhi Purple Sapphire) presented by his daughter, Mrs. Mair Jones, to the British Museum (Nat. Hist.) January 28th, 1944.

To—Whomsoever shall be the future possessor of this Amethyst

These lines are addressed in mourning before he, or she, shall assume the responsibility of owning it.**

This stone is trebly accursed and is stained with the blood, and the dishonour of everyone who has ever owned it. It was looted from the treasure of the Temple of the God Indra at Cawnpore during the Indian Mutiny in 1855 and brought to this country by Colonel W. Ferris of the Bengal Cavalry. From the day he possessed it he was unfortunate, and lost both health and money. His son who had it after his death, suffered the most persistent ill-fortune till I accepted the stone from him in 1890. He had given it once to a friend, but the friend shortly afterwards committed suicide and left it back to him by will. From the moment I had it, misfortunes attacked me until I had it bound round with a double headed snake that had been a finger ring of Heydon the Astrologer, looped up

---

* Reprinted by permission of the Trustees of the British Museum (Natural History).
** B.M. Register entry:–1944,1. Quartz (var. Amethyst), faceted, oval, (3.5 x 2.5 cm) mounted in silver ring in form of snake, decorated with zodiacal plaques and with two hinged pendants one of which bears two scarabs of amethystine quartz, the other a T in silver, engraved. Locality unknown. Mrs. Mair Jones of London by presentation January 28, 1944.

with Zodiacal plaques and neutralized between Heydon's Magic
Tau and two amethyst scarabœi of Queen Hatasu's period,
brought from Der-el-Bahari (Thebes). It remained thus quietly
until 1902, though not only I, but my wife, Professor Ross,
W. H. Rider, and Mrs. Hadden, frequently saw in my library
the Hindu Yoga, who haunts the stone trying to get it back.
He sits on his heels in a corner of the room, digging in the floor
with his hands, as if searching for it. In 1902, under protest I
gave it to a friend, who was thereupon overwhelmed with every
possible disaster. On my return from Egypt in 1903 I found
she had returned it to me, and after another great misfortune
had fallen on me I threw it into the Regent's Canal. Three
months afterwards it was brought back to me by a Wardour
St. dealer who had bought it from a dredger. Then I gave it to
a friend who was a singer, at her earnest wish. The next time
she tried to sing, her voice was dead and gone and she has
never sung since. I feel that it is exerting a baleful influence
over my new born daughter so I am now packing it in seven
boxes and depositing it at my bankers, with directions that it
is not to see the light again until I have been dead thirty three
years. Whoever shall then open it, shall first read this warning,
and then do as he pleases with the jewel. My advice to him or
her is to cast it into the sea. I am forbidden by the Rosicrucian
Oath to do this, or I would have done it long ago.

(Signed) EDWARD HERON-ALLEN
October 1904

16

Topaz Is a Blue Stone Too

When I indicated that I planned to exclude topaz from this book for reasons of brevity some of my acquaintances almost took me apart verbally. I was so impressed by their passionate feeling for the stone I began to research it. I feel fortunate that I looked deeper into the jewel box of mother earth.

A friend really set me off as a topaz trumpeter when he showed me a faceted *blue* topaz he had bought as an unset, uncut stone. It weighed twenty-four carats, was Portuguese cut, and was dazzlingly beautiful. I began to pursue the other shades of topaz. However, I had to know more about the blue topaz my friend had in his collection. He confided that he had not mined it but had bought it in a rock shop in Colorado Springs, Colorado. He bought it in the rough as a 360 carat stone with nothing but his instinct to tell him it would cut into a valuable gem. He described it as an "enormous bargain," because the people who sold it to him in the blind sale of rough gems didn't have a clue as to its worth either.

That is a fascinating rung of the gem collector's ladder. When one learns more about gemstones he begins to buy and trade. He might buy rough stones from rock shops, at gem auctions or gem sales, or he might buy stones from private individuals who have mined the stones and wish to sell them. Neither the buyer nor the seller knows EXACTLY what the worth of the stone or stones might be—but the more you learn about gemstones the less chance you have of buying one that should have been left in the ground.

Topaz, whose chemical composition is fluosilicate of aluminum, comes in the traditional yellow, pink, white, golden brown, and blue shades and, of course, colorless. It is not a minor gemstone. The blue topaz, that celestial shade that originally lured me, is often taken for aquamarine from which it may be distinguished by the more knowledgeable by its greater specific gravity. I saw a Brazilian blue topaz of 2,982 carats at the Geological Museum in London.

The Ceylon topaz was once sold for its weight in gold, so keep that in mind when you are spurning topaz as only semi-precious. The Singhalese even sold the white topazes as false diamonds and it was not difficult because they were reported to have a genius for bleaching stones like the topaz and sapphire to the point where they were mistaken for the finest diamonds. Although it was said that time restored their former hues, you will find many experts today who will tell you that topaz when properly bleached always remains colorless—or white.

The white topaz is sometimes called the "North Carolina Diamond." A friend of mine proved it by finding a beautiful white topaz at Gibson's Mine and another one at Ruth Holbrook's place. The white topaz, alas, does not hold its brilliant polish if worn regularly, but on display it is difficult for an amateur to detect the difference between it and a diamond. There are pro-diamond fans, however, who will tell you the topaz probably didn't have much fire to begin with.

I saw some colorless topaz that made me a fan of it on the spot at the Geological Museum in London. I was more attracted to it than to the rainbow hues of the brilliantly faceted zircon whose appearance so nearly approaches the diamond too. There might be some colorless topaz at Mt. Thomas in Millard County, Utah, if you wish to see it closer to home.

White topaz—"minas nova"—is a delicate pellucid gem with greater brilliancy than crystal. I have seen white topaz set in old gold and it is a sight one remembers a long time.

Don't get topaz confused with topazolite, however, as that is a topaz-yellow or green variety of *garnet*. Yellow quartz is the stone most often mistaken for topaz—and its exact mineral designation is more properly citrine than topaz. We should remember, too, that oriental topaz (so-called) is corundum, colored by oxide of iron to a sunlit, golden yellow—but it is almost pure alumina. Golden-brown shades of topaz are the most recognizable and familiar of this gem, but frequently brown quartz is also sold under the name of topaz. Red topaz is a gem that very seldom occurs naturally. It is a crimson shade with rich brown tones. It is so rare, it is taken for a variety of ruby when it does occur.

Pink topaz is probably the most beautiful of all topaz, but it is rarely if ever found in nature. It can be made from the yellow shade if you wish to home brew it. Just put the yellow topaz into the bowl of a tobacco pipe covered with sand to pack it in, and ashes. A small amount of heat will change the stone to a glorious pastel pink. In spite of the beauty of the pink stone the topaz followers always seem to seek out the traditional golden shade with its warming hues.

It is very difficult to find a flawless topaz, as the stone is likely to have inclusions, so if you do chance upon a true, clear topaz in your gem hunt you have a gem of, not only good price, but of special beauty dimensions as well.

Be certain you entrust your topaz to a gemologist who understands the stone perfectly so that its clear beauty is respected in both cutting and setting. The luster of a well-cut topaz is a delight.

You may feel you have been unprotected in your jewelry buying forays when you discover what has been offered as topaz. How often has someone shown me a necklace of citrine (yellow quartz) and insisted it was topaz!

Topaz received its name from the island in the Red Sea variously described as Topaza, Topazos, and Topazion. Topazos, now called Zebirget (Island of St. John) was derived from the Greek *topazein*, to guess. Like most of the names that have come down to us from the ancients, it makes much more sense than the ones we invent for shock appeal today. Pliny says topaz was originally found on Topaza and it received the name because the island was surrounded by fog so often it was difficult to find. Mariners gave it the name because they had to GUESS they had reached it.

Most of us know that topaz is the birthstone for November, a right, crisp month for this warm stone with its comforting, blazing beauty. Someone confused me by saying that Pliny originally gave the name topaz to the *yellow-hued* peridot found on Topaza. (Just as all green stones were called emerald, so any stone that was yellow-toned and transparent was likely to be called a topaz. Then it was a loosely applied term, but it firmed into its present name in modern times when instruments and other checks separated one gemstone from another.) Since Peridot has always been *green* with only a golden eye, I would think it would have been the emerald rather than the topaz of the ancients.

It is amazing how often in the annals of history the poets have remembered the topaz when they wanted to speak of a gem with warm, rich, and lustrous tones. I, as a quasi-poet, have always thought my mother was the only woman in the world outside of a portrait who had topaz eyes.

As many of us know, the Breast Plate of Aaron was divided into first, second, third, and fourth rows—*primus ordo, secundus ordo, tertius ordo*, and *quartus ordo*—and topaz is *primus ordo*. That would seem to vindicate my friends who clamored for topaz to be given a hearing. Topaz seems to be a stone whose price does not vary much in the larger sizes. This is due to the fact that it has been found in all sizes and therefore a large stone is not that much rarer than a small one.

If you are able to find and examine some of the French jewelry of the nineteenth century you will see that extraordinary things can be done with topaz in necklaces, earrings, pins, and other jewelry. It is a particularly lovely stone to use with enameling. Did you ever think how enameling seems to add the illusion of additional gemstones when it is used properly in jewelry design? Golden topaz becomes gold on gold when it is put in that setting, and few precious stones look as splendid as when that coupling is made.

Although specifically listed as a semi-precious gem, topaz is one of the gems of history that wrings enormous respect and affection from its admirers. The entire species of the topaz represent gems of quality and stability but stones from certain sources have perishable color and too much sunlight can fade them considerably. Topaz generates positive electricity, and its lure as a gem to topaz-lovers would demonstrate this. I personally favor pink topaz over the more familiar yellow— and, of course, the beautiful blue topaz to which I have been exposed makes me feel I have seen the blue shade at its best. One of the charms, or perhaps the snares, of writing a book of this character is that one sells oneself so completely on the entire gemstone kingdom it appears difficult to holiday at anything except surface mining for the rest of one's life.

I have been overwhelmed by the extraordinary stones my mining companions have found on excursions other than our ruby and sapphire safari. If you would like to know what might be ahead of you as a topaz collector here are some of the gorgeous shades of the gemstone collected by my friends as they named them to me. Besides the blue topaz that was bought (but mined by someone else), they found "cherry topaz, golden topaz, had a ring made from two rhodolite garnets and one white topaz, another ring made from a single large white topaz." They have had jewelry of every description made from the gemstone, laced with other stones—bracelets, necklaces, earrings, tie tacks, rings, pendants on necklaces, clasps on pearl necklaces, and pins. I have viewed both the set and the unset stones and have come away dazzled, and with an understanding of my friend, who can not only not resist the lure of a mining expedition but whose involvement with gemstones is so deep his eye can detect a possible gem treasure at a mass gem sale the way Ruth Holbrook's quick glance can pry a ruby loose from the Cowee Valley soil.

Topaz, like so many other gem materials, is found in pegmatites, pegmatite dikes, and in cavities in granite. It occurs as the result of the action of hot acid vapors upon rocks rich in aluminum silicates. The glittering face of topaz may also be one of the linings of lithophysae. These are rock shells having empty spaces between them resulting from gas bubbles. Lithophysae is taken from the Greek words for "stone bubble."

It is interesting to note that topaz, whose hardness is 8 on Mohs' Scale, can be found in placer deposits. It is one of those heavier minerals that remain reasonably stationary as other, lighter stones are swept away or broken up by weathering. The standard Moh's Scale of Hardness is shown in one of the chapters on ruby and sapphire but I shall repeat it for reference here, inserting some stones you might find and their approximate rank in hardness.

1. Talc

2. Gypsum

2.5 Jet and Amber

3. Calcite

3.5 Coral

4. Pearl—Fluorite

5. Apatite

6. Lapis Lazuli
   Turquoise
   Opal
   Orthoclase
   Moonstone

6.5 Peridot
    Jade (Nephrite)

7. Jadeite
Amethyst (Quartz)
Onyx
Chalcedony
Bloodstone

7.5 Tourmaline
Zircon

7.75 Emerald

8. Topaz—Aquamarine
Spinel

8.5 Chrysoberyl

8.8 Ruby (corundum)

9. Sapphire (corundum)

10. Diamond

Lest you think the topaz has no legends to its name, it does. The topaz was thought to be one of the original tonics as it was believed it could heal the sick if put into wine.

A friend mentioned that some topaz of not too fine quality for gems was found in a small community near Round Oak, Georgia, where a new road was cut. "I dug along the top soil," she said, "and found some nice stones for my collection, but the Rock Hound Club, of which I am a member, did it more extensively and used pick axes as they were mining in rock beds. I stuck to soil."

Another friend said he found "smoky topaz" in the same area in which he found rose amethyst—at a mining site near Highlands where we stayed during our ruby mining days. Although he was a specialist in gems I questioned the possibility of its being smoky topaz at that site and he promised to check out its properties in a special test. So many things that look yellow or brown are called topaz it has become a gemstone for which one always asks credentials.

In Georgia, topaz has been found by gold miners in the gravels of the Etowah, Chattahoochee Rivers and the Chestatee River, which is in North Central Georgia. This latter river has its origin in White County, runs across the eastern part of Lumpkin County and empties into Lake Lanier, north of Gainesville, Georgia. It flows just east of Dahlonega, the gold site. The largest piece of topaz ever found there was the size of a huge egg. It was cut, in part, into a striking brilliant. Stow, in Oxford County, Maine has some topaz, and southern Utah has some yellow, blue, and colorless stones. I saw a blue topaz (from Brazil) of 2,982 carats that was the same turquoise shade as my friend bought at his bargain sale.

Topaz may be found in Granville County in North Carolina and on Mountain Creek and Bowling Mountain. There are many other areas of the United States where topaz may be found; and Mexico has some white topaz. The son of our ruby safari leader found a white topaz of good quality at Ruth Holbrook's place. It was very pure and brilliant-cut into three treasured stones.

You might have luck scouting it in New England if you are near Coos County in New Hampshire or Carroll County, Conway, and Baldface Mountain in that state. Try Mason County in Texas, Colorado Springs or Pikes Peak in Colorado. Also Devil's Head, Douglas County, is a good spot, and San Diego in California and the Little Three Mine near Ramona in California. Sagadahoc County and Androscoggin County in Maine are other areas where you might run across topaz. There has been topaz taken from Virginia mines near Amelia and also from Topaz Cove near Jerico, Utah, Fairfield County, Connecticut, and Chesterfield County, South Carolina. If you are going in a Canadian direction you might try York County in New Brunswick. If you would like to see some Brazilian quartz that looks like topaz you might try the Astro Minerals Limited on East 34th Street in New York City. They have only foreign stones, but for seventy-five cents a carat you can buy yourself a very colorful stone. The lighter hue is only fifty cents a carat and well cut.

I think you will find less precious topaz in the United States than some of the other gems you will search out but be cautious, even in your surface mining. Remember the lesson of that great mineralogist who lived in the first century, Pliny the Elder. He died in an attempt to view the eruption of Mount Vesuvius. To paraphrase Mr. Truman—when the heat is too great, you have to know when to get out of the volcano.

17

✢

Jade—Gem of the Ages!

Jade has such oriental connotations it is difficult to think of it locally. Actually jade is two stones, the minerals jadeite and nephrite. Nephrite is the ancient jade we know, and jadeite, the lovely gem jade, has only been worked in China since the eighteenth century. Although I had once been told that jade "has not been mined in China for centuries," there is no actual proof that jade has ever been found in China at any time according to scholars today. Chinese Turkestan is the home of nephrite and the earth bed of some of the loveliest jade carvings one could find.

Jadeite comes in a preferred shade that is the color of a rich emerald but jade generally comes in every shade of the rainbow—it may be white, violet, lilac, red-brown, black, yellow-brown, mauve, orange, green, and white, and I have also seen some marbled patterns that were impressive. However, imperial jade, as the emerald green hue is called, is exquisite and received its name from an Empress of China who demanded every piece of jade found be shown to her. Her collection numbered thousands of carvings. She is one acquisitionist I totally understand. People who collect jade love it for life. One of the most appealing ornaments on earth is a gracefully carved jade goddess. I am always searching for one . . . more.

Since the hardness of jade (nephrite 6½, jadeite 7) lies far from that of the diamond, it is astonishing to learn that this stone is the *hardiest* of all gemstones. Due to its unique matted structure—its felted fibers—it is a difficult object to break. Nephrite has greater compressive strength than steel, and that gives a good reason why there was so much interest in an anvil that was made of jade—and apparently used for more than an ornament.

Although jadeite is the rarer of the two kinds of jade the distinction between them is a difficult test for the eye alone. Don't worry if the jade you find looks too large to be valuable, or even jade. A boulder of nephrite weighing over half a ton (1,156 pounds) has been found, and you may see it in the British Museum of Natural History in London. It comes from Batagol, Irkutsk, Siberia. Dr. G. F. Kunz found a piece weighing over two tons so it is THERE, and you most likely won't need a compound microscope to find it. This stone is usually found in boulders that have been waterworn. Prehistoric man used jade for tools and weapons. A simple ax might have taken ten years of painstaking carving with abrasives to become usable. It is thought that Eastern man may have had a jade age comparable to the flint age of Western man.

Even scholars know very little about jade. As a precious stone it was the first thing stolen from graves. Also, jade carving was perfected early and has changed little through the centuries, so it is hard to date exactly. The most accurate way to determine the age of a piece of jade is by the style of its carving. The earliest pieces were quite formalized. The later pieces had considerably more individualism. Grave robbers, however, separated the stolen jade from their burial sites and laced the pieces through the market in such a way there was no chance to know where it specifically came from—so many pieces of old, old jade have never been identified positively.

When I was studying the contents of the Avery Brundage Collection of Oriental Art in the De Young Museum at San Francisco, California a few years ago I became quite interested in jade and the idea of using powdered jade to cure physical ills. Also, the Chinese believe that if jade is powdered and mixed with water and taken just before death the ritual will prevent decomposition. Imagine! Jeweled medicine to keep the bloom on the rose that is you.

Jade has long been considered to be connected with good fortune. Its Chinese name is Yu, actually meaning gem, but a term that has become synonymous with the best of everything, the ultimate. To the Chinese, jade is a sacred bridge between heaven and earth, embodying the five cardinal virtues of Wisdom, Justice, Charity, Modesty, and Courage. The Orientals revere jade so deeply it is not surprising to find the Chinese consider jade the prototype of all gems.

The Brundage collection has the most comprehensive display of jade in the world—covering more than four thousand years from neolithic times to today. The Western name of the stone—jade—is also derived from good fortune but it is of medical origin. Cortez found Indians wearing jade next to their skin to relieve colic or side pains. The gemstone was valued so highly by the Aztecs that they hid it from the Spaniards, allowing them to take the less highly prized gold. The Spanish call it *piedras de hijada* or "stones of the side." Jade, of course, is a corruption of the Spanish.

Also in the Brundage Collection are ancient bronze mirrors bearing the good luck wish: "May you always drink from jade springs."

The Chinese always used jade for gifts of good omen. To give someone a gift of a jade carving of mountains, the symbol of longevity, was to wish him long life. At one time jade butterflies were buried with the dead to ensure immortality. A jade carving of five bats, the Chinese symbol of happiness, represents the five happinesses—wealth, old age, health, natural death, and love of virtue.

There are twelve hundred pieces in the jade display at the museum. There's a two-thousand-year-old, seven-and-one-half-inch long greenish-brown water buffalo from the Han Dynasty; a three-inch by five-inch dragon pendant in light green and beige jade from approximately the time of the Warring States in the fourth century B.C.; a Pi-T'ung or bowl-type brush holder for use of scholars made in the late Ming

Dynasty of the sixteenth century. The brilliant, dark green object is seven inches high and eight inches in diameter with an outer surface bearing many sharply carved figures. The jade collection is one of the most comprehensive in existence— ranging from the earliest known jade sculpture to more modern, tediously carved jade bowls.

There is one figure in the collection, a superb jade gentleman (lohan), among the treasures. It is an eleven-inch Ching Dynasty figure that was carved by Chinese artisans who used century-old methods: a bamboo stylus and the abrasive action of sand and water. This piece is so perfect it almost moves.

The Chinese wear jade on the neck and on the breast. Oriental businessmen have been known to hold jade amulets in their hands to counsel them. Jade has had many powers attributed to it. It was considered a bringer of rain and believed to be able to drive off wild spirits. According to E. A. Wallis Budge in *Amulets and Talismans*, "It cured dropsy, abolished thirst, made a man victorious in battle, protected from lightning and relieved palpitation of the heart." Shades of Albert the Great.

I believe jade is carved today much as it was centuries ago. Now two men operate a wire saw while a third man applies "black dust," powdered carborundum, which actually does the cutting, as it is an abrasive. Because it is sturdy in spite of its relative softness, it is a good stone for carving. It has been made into everything from boxes to bangles.

Hong Kong today is the center of the world jade market but the earliest shipments came from Siberia and Chinese Turkestan, where it was mined and loaded on camels to start its long journey to the talented hands of the artisans who would make it into objects to be remembered as long as beauty is revered. Marco Polo reports having seen jade caravans in the thirteenth century as they entered the jade gate, a pass in the Great Wall of China. Presumably some of the jade in those caravans is on view at the De Young Museum. If jade is your special gem and you are near San Francisco the Avery Brundage Collection there is a delicious taste of the past.

Did you know there was a California Jade Rush? It apparently happened in 1950 but unearthed few pieces of good jade. California jade is likely to be white or grayish green. Monterey County, Cape San Martin, or El Dorado County, California, are possible places where you might find some jade. Wyoming has been called the best jade area in the United States—if there is any left. Flawless, remarkably fine jade of the nephrite variety has been found there. Try Sweetwater there. Also Carbon and Natrona counties. Jade might be found in northwestern Alaska—Jade Mountain in the Kobuk region. Also seek out Yavapai County in Arizona. Additionally in California you might try Humboldt, Kern, Marin, and Mendocino counties—also Placer, Sacramento, San Benito, San Luis Obispo, Siskiyou, Trinity, Tulare; Park, Saguache, Teller, Colorado; Curry, Oregon; Wasco, Oregon; Custer, South Dakota, and Wausau, Wisconsin. Lytton in British Columbia might be a productive place to explore.

If you are thinking of finding something that can be made into an heirloom of practically indestructible dimensions here is a stone you might pursue. Unfortunately it is not one you will be likely to find on your way to the movies—but, like the other gemstones, it is there. If you make jade the object of your special search, you will have a stone of great duration, and the possibility of building a collection of jade objects to rival an emperor's.

A sad thing about modern civilization is that so much hope has been lifted from it, so many wonderful fantasies are absent, so many promises for tomorrow are unmade. But one can always look *back* with pleasure if the future seems too bleak. Take this single thing out of the past that is still with us, exquisite jade, and think of all the things that surround its history. If you remember only one, that the Chinese considered jade a step toward achieving immortality, or that if enough powdered jade were swallowed one could become immortal . . . how CAN you have a dull day thinking thoughts like that?

18

❦

Quartz ... Here and There

It isn't surprising to many of us to find that quartz, which is the commonest of all minerals, makes up about twelve percent of the earth's crust. It is found in every class of rock and forms under an enormous variety of conditions. There is hardly a color you could name that is not represented in the quartz spectrum. The chapter on amethyst gave a few hints about this mineral, but since it has many sides there is room for additional observation about it.

When one thinks of the rock crystal of the Herkimer Diamonds and other colorless quartz it is surprising to learn that quartz is used by scientists to control frequency in electronic devices. I believe this is because it possesses something known as piezoelectricity. When pressure is applied to this mineral in the right direction an electric current is set up. Quartz has been used in walkie-talkies, among other things, and is a mineral that has an enormous industrial importance that would take many pages to salute.

As a stone of gem value it has given us the exquisite amethyst and the quite rare blush tones of rose quartz. It isn't quite understood why the prolific quartz mineral has not produced more of the beautiful rose quartz shade. This is, as we mentioned, one of the gemstones that shows asterism. You might find this lovely pink-cheeked stone in Newry, Maine, but no one can promise that every piece of rose quartz you find will have a star in it. The opposite is more likely.

Quartz has a simplicity of composition, the crystallized

silica, oxide of silicon. Quartz occurs as the colorless, transparent rock crystal, as milky quartz with its white, nearly opaque form, and as smoky quartz with its grays, browns, and yellows, as well as a garden of other shades. This mineral is so devoid of color in its rock crystal state it was formerly considered a form of petrified water. The usual metallic oxides that color other gemstones might be responsible for the shades in quartz. The answer simply isn't known.

It is sad to note that the gloriously delicate face of rose quartz, which is rose-red or pink in shade, may fade when exposed to strong sunlight. However, if you can find this quite rare, delightful shade of quartz you will think of nothing but how you can keep it with you as a delightful stone to have or to hold. While quartz is quite hard—7—it is also brittle, but it is considered a hardy stone like the diamond. It stands up magnificently to changing conditions, with the exception of color changes such as the exposure of rose quartz to intense sunlight.

Yellow quartz is one of the gem minerals most often taken for some other stone. Actually yellow quartz is called citrine but it is what most stores will offer as "topaz." Only recently have I seen signs under "topaz" advertised stones signifying it as "(quartz)." People have been responsible for the large sales of quartz as topaz in the past because they have been quite resistant about calling a golden stone anything but topaz.

You are not too likely to mistake a piece of colorless quartz for a diamond, however, as the latter has a very high index of refraction, which accounts for its brilliancy when properly cut to advantage this characteristic. A certain kind of green quartz has even been mistaken for jade, but many, many stones have been in that caravan, including hornblende and a kind of garnet and the more likely soapstone.

One of the most provocative names in the mineral kingdom is the Desert Rose. This is a mineral which has a rosette form and which was originally represented to me as quartz, which it is not. I find it is calcium sulphate but delightful in any mineral category. Once one peeps into the jeweled vaults that are all around us he wants to write about gemstones until his fingers fall numb—but even then he would have missed most of the magic that surrounds the stones. It is sad that so much that might be told about so many beautiful stones must be left out of this book. At best, such exquisite earth poetry as the peridot, the tourmaline, the alexandrite, jade, lapis lazuli, zircon, carnelian, and turquoise will receive only shallow recognition.

When you begin to follow the trail of these crystallized or solidified flowers the earth produces and has produced for millions of years, you will find many, many more "favorite" stones than I have selected—but for the moment perhaps these lines will make you want to know them better.

Rose quartz is the shade of quartz most desired and you might find it in Saratoga County in New York. New England has some rose quartz as we mentioned earlier. Also, La Grange, Georgia, is the spot where a friend found asteriated rose quartz. Diamond Hill in Cumberland Township, Rhode Island, has quartz. Portland, Connecticut, Chester and Delaware counties in Pennsylvania have quartz. If you go across the border to the north you might find quartz in Chester, Lunenburg County and Nova Scotia . . . and there is more than a small chance you will because Nova Scotia is noted for its many varieties of quartz. Kingston in Frontenac County, Ontario is also a possibility for finding this commonest of all minerals.

White quartz veins are considered good guides to gold deposits in certain regions so don't be too sure that your quartz expeditions won't turn into a gold rush.

19

✌

Lapis Lazuli

An Always New Ancient Stone

This stone almost surely was the "sapphire" of the ancients. But that isn't to say Catherine the Great of Russia did not put it to extravagant use as well. She had the walls of a ballroom made entirely of lapis lazuli. Considering its intense blue tones, that must have been a difficult background for the ladies of the court to dress up—or down—to. I think Jezebel, in her ivory room, showed more exacting, if not exciting, taste.

Lapis lazuli has been called a rock. It is always found in association with limestone which has been impregnated by the action of some intrusive igneous rock. It is practically opaque, which accounts for its never being faceted.

The most famous repository of lapis lazuli is at the mines of Badakshan in Afghanistan. These mines have been worked for thousands of years, always impregnably protected. Russia has some lapis. I saw some from Sludianka in the Lake Baikal region of the U.S.S.R. Gunnison County in Colorado is one of the few places in the United States where lapis lazuli might be found.

This gem rock with a name like lyric poetry has dimensions of awesome beauty, and should be better known than it is. Its shade is deep and gorgeous and somehow commits one to it however briefly she is exposed to its blue mysteries. The most ancient lapis has a telling personality, and its bright face doesn't seem to fade. It has been used at all periods of history from prehistoric times. I have viewed lapis lazuli scarabs from the Old Egyptian Kingdom (XII and XIII Dynasty), to very recent specimens. And I have seen lively lapis lazuli that was found with calcined bones in a Hittite Period "burial" from the late seventh century B.C.

I keep running into lapis lazuli in far corners of the world. I saw a beautiful old piece set in a gold ring at the Victoria and Albert Museum in London, and it was as bright as tomorrow. The Louvre in Paris has a worthy collection of lapis. There is a rather large table there set with many interesting stones—including lapis lazuli. That Paris treasure box also has covered lapis jars encrusted with jewels and gold bands, small urns, bowls, and many varieties of compotes made of lapis. It was not generally made into boxes—covered boxes—but I did find one exquisite example of just that. It was a tiny square treasure of a box with gold mounts set with a miniature of Maximilian I, King of Bavaria. I made a hard wish that it could be mine.

Through the ages lapis lazuli has been fashioned into rings, vases, and many forms of ornamental wear. The intense blue color was the raw material for the glorious marine colors in many ancient paintings as well. It was especially popular as an amulet, and the early amuletic forms were interesting because they were shaped to their individual meaning, that is, amulets in the form of parts of the body protected those parts.

The Sumarians of antiquity believed anyone who carried the lapis lazuli as an amulet carried a god with him. Beautiful scarabs were made from lapis, and beads were made from the paste mixed from powdered lapis lazuli. However, the beads I came across are not generally dramatic and one wonders why lapis is used in such bland creations of neckwear. One particular necklace I remember was interspersed with white quartz, deadening the bright blue eye of the stone beyond belief. When one considers what can be done with a tiny lapis bowl mounted in ormolu, the wisdom of "beading" seems to be in question. However, someone told me of a necklace of lapis lazuli, a double strand of it, with a jade clasp that is very, very lovely—and it must be for it has a price tag of $25,000.

There is a piece of lapis lazuli in the Avery Brundage Collection of Oriental Art in the De Young Museum in San Francisco that is a delight. The brilliant blue lapis lazuli was often treated by the ancient Chinese as a pictorial medium. The Ching Dynasty piece I happened upon is nine and a half inches high and thirteen inches wide. It portrays a favorite subject, a mountain with tortuous trails, bridges, running water, and wind-whipped trees. It is very, very real at the same time you think you might have dreamed it.

A rock hound friend of mine has a piece of lapis lazuli that looks like a tiny, beautiful Christmas tree. This is another case of where a rock or gem collector executed a good swap-or-sell program as he tells me he paid only thirty dollars for the piece, which is, indeed, very, very beautiful.

Lapis lazuli is one of the gems that is striking in its own earthy dress but decorated with gold or coupled with either white or imperial jade it must become a combination of color music one would long remember. The gem kingdom is a world of surprising beauty and we would do ourselves a service in refreshing our spirits just browsing through the gems of history in a museum.

It is my understanding, large, well-colored specimens of lapis lazuli are so rare lapis is seldom used for bowls and vases of any size. I can attest to that because most of the lapis ornaments I have seen were almost miniature. The lapis lazuli in most modern ornaments is a thin veneer cemented onto metal. That is a pity, for it is a brilliantly colored reminder that the flowers of the earth never die, and the lapis I have seen from eras to which I had been a stranger is proof of that.

If you cannot find lapis lazuli in the best United States spot, which is Italian Mountain in Gunnison County, Colorado, where it is deep shaded and as prized as the treasure of Afghanistan, you may find the lighter, weaker-hued lapis near Upland in San Bernardino, California, at Cascade Canyon.

Wherever you find its bright eye consider yourself a lucky miner. It is a gem of unquenchable beauty!

20

❧

Turquoise

A Persian Promise That Is at Home in America

Even if I were not a quasi-poet I know I would become slightly lyrical at the sight and touch of most gemstones, but some forms of pale turquoise are the exception. They have always reminded me of Cracker Jack box souvenirs. However, I know now what a truly beautiful stone it can be and how much it deserves its followers, so here are a few facts and fancies for the turquoise contingent to nibble on.

The fascination with turquoise is an old one—it goes back to prehistoric days. The spider web pattern that veils the stone is considered one of the marks of authentic turquoise, but I find myself becoming more and more interested in the darker variety, not just as a gem for jewelry but as a solid background of beauty for such things as wall plaques or picture frames. To produce the darker, lovelier shade of turquoise the Persians soaked (and still do) the lighter shade of turquoise in butter.

The most colorful temple to turquoise is the mausoleum and domed mosque of Ali, the son-in-law of Mohammed, near Al Kufah in Iraq. It is the largest, surely, and the most exquisite salute to the turquoise gemstone ever created. Beautiful beyond the tongue's power of praise, it sits outlined against the Mazar-i-Sharif sky of almost equal hue. One of the most graceful edifices, and certainly the most poetically colorful, ever built.

Turquoise, for most of us living in the United States, is associated more closely with the American Indian than with the ancients. Even today it is the stone from which they fashion many of their jewelry souvenirs.

The word turquoise would seem to come from the French for "Turkish," as the stones reached Europe by way of Turkey after they left Persia. Actually the name is derived from the Chaldean, *torkeja*, meaning Turkey.

The Buddhists associate this particular stone with Buddha because he is said to have overcome a hideous monster with the help of a turquoise stone.

The finest turquoise in the world still comes from the famous deposits near Nishpur in the Iranian province of Khorassan. Some of the turquoise I have seen from Iran with gilt inscriptions is very, very lovely and of the warm, rich shade which surely seems to have been soaked in some of nature's magic to retain such magnificent hues.

Turquoise is an opaque stone whose color ranges from sky blue or greenish blue to apple green. Since the stone is porous, and it is massive and seldom found in crystal form (except in Virginia) it needs care and grooming. Even the sweat glands of the skin affect it. If it is exposed, immersed in liquids or unclean matter, it risks losing its bright color to startlingly unattractive shadings. It is a mineral of arid climates. However, the water contained in the stone is important to it and when expelled results in some of the unsightly changes of color described.

The *color* of turquoise is something that has always reached me and it seems to reach most people. There are little magics in this stone and of course it is all in the color. Color does influence outline and can put you off or draw you to it. Therefore, if the shade of gemstone you are wearing is not right for you it is better that you put it into your Riker Mount or give it to your last enemy—after you have convinced yourself it is positively not YOUR cup of mineral tea.

Gold seems to be a very proper setting for turquoise, although most of the American Indian jewelry one sees is made with silver mountings and frames. Turquoise is a shade that flatters most people, brightens and lightens them. With gold it is so elegant, with silver it is a bit more casual—more daytime. But—it can be a very memorable part of your day at the mines. This opaque stone, which has maintained its popularity over thousands of years, has had endearing qualities for every generation whether it was seen as sky blue, apple green, or the rarer robin's egg blue.

Turquoise is a near-to-the-surface stone, so you won't have to bring your own bulldozer when you pursue it. As with most mining areas, though, be certain you get permission to mine or there could be difficulties of possession afterward.

Turquoise matrix is turquoise itself because it is so completely part of the stone it could not be separated from it without destruction to the gem. Although the Iranian or Persian matrix (or mother rock) is black (the Iranian turquoise is the most expensive) the turquoise matrix in the United States runs from brown to white.

The turquoise did not escape having therapeutic or prophylactic qualities associated with it. The Arabs called it *Firuzaj* or "the lucky stone," and prize it today as they formerly did. The idea that it protects the wearer from poison and snakebite and eye diseases might be expected of a gem for whom people for thousands of years have felt great affection; but the fact that it warns an owner of the approach of death by changing color is a test of courage. Can you imagine how a stone like that could spoil a Sunday picnic? You are about to bite into that herb-fried chicken and you look down at the turquoise ring on your hand and it isn't the same shade it was when you left home in the morning. Well, sir, you aren't likely to enjoy that mouthful of fowl, nor the ride home!

With that legend in mind we might suggest that you do not expose your turquoise stone to strong light or it may fade and you won't know whether IT is going or YOU are leaving the scene—permanently.

Turquoise is generally cut en cabochon which, incidentally, has been said to come from the French *caboche*, meaning knob or pate. Chemically, it is a phosphate of copper and aluminum and is frequently found with copper.

The beautiful, dark shade of turquoise is not plentiful and comes in quite small pieces. If you do see a very large piece it may mean, I have been told, that it has been treated.

Turquoise lacks the luster of most gems and many do not take a high polish—but its hue is unimpaired by candlelight. Be careful of exposing your turquoise to dry air, because as turquoise loses its moisture it turns greener.

The best turquoise is seldom exported as it is so highly prized where it is mined. The finest quality turquoise is called Turquois Vielle Roche, uniform and compact in texture and highly prized in Iranian and Mohammedan states. If someone wants to give you Turquois Nouvelle Roche, turn from it. This is doubtful turquoise to say the least. It is generally supposed to be a fossil bone colored by phosphate of iron. If you wish to make a test of the two varieties . . . the Nouvelle Roche always effervesces in acid, which has no effect on true turquoise. I have seen odontolite, called bone turquoise, which is the fossilized teeth of extinct creatures. The specimens I saw were blue, pure, and lovely. Imitations of true turquoise are fairly translucent and lose their color tone by candlelight. Also they are much softer than the original.

The Sinai Peninsula, which is considerably more than a bus ride away, has turquoise. I'd suggest you try Nye City, Nevada, or Los Cerillos, New Mexico, which are nearer. For variety you have San Bernardino County, California, and Sierra Nevada, Nevada, as possible turquoise sources. Lander County near Cortez, in Nevada, is a good spot to check. The Sierra Blanca Mountains in Texas have yielded some turquoise. You may find some green turquoise in Elko County, Nevada, if you have a taste for a cooler shade of it. Jefferson and Clay counties in Alabama and Manassa in Colorado might have some. Santa Fe County and Grant County are also possibles in New Mexico. If the New Mexico pickings are thin there is good reason for it as they have been extensively mined. Morenci, Arizona, is a good spot. Bisbee and Courtland in Cochise County, Arizona, might surprise you with a turquoise stone you will cherish.

21

࿔

Zircon—the Near Diamond!

This is a mineral that is always in crystal form. The colorless and the blue zircon are the most familiar, but there are also brown, ruddy red, gray, and green. Practically all zircons are heat treated to give them a desirable color. The reddish-brown stones are heated to extremely high temperatures. When a closed container is used, the stones change to the desired blue or colorless; but when air is allowed to flow through the container, the stones become the cherished golden-yellow or a red shade. Occasionally "hotting up" zircons results in the stone reverting to undistinguished shades.

This is a gem in which asteriation is unlikely. Oddly, because it is not a precious gem, but a lovely semi-precious one, the zircon is the one stone which may be mistaken for the diamond with good reason. Like the diamond, it has individual fires of its own, and with proper faceting they will burst upon the eye with incredible beauty. The zircon may be represented to you as a diamond, but you are not likely to find a synthetic zircon because there are none. The zircon is quite brittle although it is as hard as tourmaline, 7.5 on Mohs' Scale —and its faceted edges do not stand up too well as evidenced by frequent chipping. One of the ways to tell a diamond from a zircon generally is the fact that the zircon has double refraction. You really need help in identifying gemstones if you want to be absolutely *sure*.

The name of the zircon species is very, very old. You can have your choice of the Arabic *zarqun* or the Persian *zargun*, meaning vermilion and gold-colored respectively. In reading old books on old stones the words jacinth and hyacinth, by which the zircon was known anciently, turned up repeatedly, so this is a stone for which the ancients had much feeling. And at the present time they are names given to the red to brown zircon. You will find the name *jargoons* given to zircons that range from colorless to pale yellow.

The jacinth was known as the gem of fidelity. And as hyacinth (with no relation to the flower at all), it drove away evil spirits and bad dreams as an amulet, and protected men against fascination, lightning; it fortified the heart, restored the appetite, produced sleep, and banished grief and melancholy from the mind. (I still like the games the ancients played.) If only all the mixed-up people in the world would go gem hunting it seems most of the ills of creation would be put away for another day. And in searching out a zircon you might run into something that occurs in Africa, where zircon crystals have been found within a diamond.

The sapphire we know today was sometimes called hyacinth during Pliny's time. However, gemstones have been sorted out sufficiently now and their composition has been broken down to such a point there is little chance of final miscalculations by experts.

Here's a stone you might find in beach sands—eastern Florida is a good place to look. Specimens might also be found in heavy sands in North Carolina. Also, one may find loose crystals in Henderson County, North Carolina. You might also find zircon in New Jersey in Sparta and Natural Bridge. New York is another possibility. El Paso County, Colorado, should have zircon—try St. Peter's Dome there. But, Ontario in Canada has produced zircons of remarkably good size. Some crystals up to a foot in length have been found there. However, like all things that are oversized, the purity of the crystals found do not compare with the size, and the clear gems obtained are minuscule in comparison, leaning toward a carat or two in weight. Renfrew County is the exact spot there on which to concentrate, however. It isn't likely you will come away emptyhanded. In Quebec in Canada you might try the Hull County area and also Argenteuil County.

22

❧

Peridot—Gem with a Golden Eye

Peridot has to be one of the most discriminating greens in the spectrum. Peridot is another name (the gemstone name) for dark green olivine. Chrysolite is the name given to stones of yellowish-green olivine. Peridot is a magnesium-iron silicate. Although it has a definite bottle-green hue, shadings toward green-gold and green-rust are likely. One could say peridot is generally green with a golden eye. It has frequently been called the "Evening Emerald," due to its gorgeous shading. It isn't possible to praise it enough.

This is a stone that was originally confused with the ancient topaz, as the old mineralogists tended to use more instinct than science to identify specimens, and grouped them according to color. Also, the large peridot stones came from the island of Zebirget or St. John's Island in the Red Sea, which is believed to be the same island that produced the "topaz" of Pliny's time. Years ago, peridot was called topaz since the gems came from Topazos, now known as Zebirget.

It is a gemstone that is rather soft (measuring 6½ on Mohs' Scale of Hardness) therefore it is not put into settings likely to be scratched. The step form of cutting is suggested for the stone, although it is sometimes cut round or oval.

The ferrous iron in this stone accounts for its color and the olive tint in its arises from oxidation of the iron.

Peridot, with its beauty, femininity, and grace is a likely high-fashion stone. French jewelers have shown a great preference for it. What greater nod to its fashion face can one introduce than that, since the French have been giving us exquisite gem settings for a very long time.

Put it against the snow white of an evening gown, the milk shade of a woman's throat. Wear it if you are black-haired, redheaded, or a pale blonde and it will belong to you in dazzling fashion notes. There is something smart AND beautiful about peridot. Perhaps it is the combination of its shade and the step cut that is so often done to expose its color ceiling. In any event, this is one of the stones that has as much "class" as an emerald so don't hestitate to pursue the peridot wherever it might be waiting for you to discover its flirtatious eye. I believe one of the most impressive specimens of peridot is in Cologne Cathedral in Germany in the Shrine of the Magi there.

A gem of legend, the peridot has been said to be a stone of friendship and to have the power to keep the mind free from envy—but envied *you* will be if you find peridot in the following possible spots. Gila County in Arizona has some, and it is doubted that you will encounter the Gila Monster while you dig for the gemstone there. There should also be some peridot very near Globe, in stream gravels. Also, like the garnet, this is a stone likely to be found on anthills—try Holbrook, Arizona. And, Afton, New Mexico, has peridot—look into Kilbourne Hole there, and also Buell Park, McKinley County. The San Carlos Indian Reservation is worth penetrating. My friends found beautiful peridot specimens on that Reservation in Arizona. One was four carats and was cut into a brilliant. They consider this location the finest in the country for peridot. It is surrounded by Globe on the southwest, Morenci on the southeast and Show Low on the north. You might have luck at Webster, Jackson County, North Carolina. And if you want to trod on peridot, how about Hawaii with its peridot sand? Also, Timothy Mountain in British Columbia might yield more than just scenery.

It matters not where you find this green poetry as its golden eye will be a delicious memory for you long after you have taken it from its earthy home.

23

❧

Tourmaline—Stone of a Hundred Hues

Tourmaline is a gemstone in the silicate classification, and is of such complex construction that John Ruskin made that frequently quoted remark about it: "The chemistry of it is more like a medieval doctor's prescription than the making of a respectable mineral."

This stone is known for its variety of hue. Its color range is awesome—green, blue, red, yellow, brown, and black in shades of pink, amethyst, rose, grape, and colorless.

Some crystals of tourmaline are of more than one color and stones of mixed colors can be cut from these. Pink and green are a relatively common combination of this phenomenon and when the color mixing shows the core color of the crystal overlaid by another color or even additional colors it is called "watermelon tourmaline." In any event it is a sight for any eye hungry for beauty and a gem one would not be likely to throw back no matter how small the specimen.

Tourmaline comes from the Ceylonese word *turmali,* and was first used when a packet of the gemstones was brought from Amsterdam to Ceylon in the eighteenth century. In Ceylon, oddly, the term is used to identify the yellow zircon. Someone told me the term *turmali* means "parcel of mixed stones." That seems apt.

Tourmaline is usually found in pegmatite dikes of granites, wherever coarse granitic rocks and their related pegmatite dikes come to the surface.

Something somewhat peculiar to tourmaline is that each of the colors seems to have a different name—rubellite, indicolite, and dravite being a few, but they all add up to gem tourmaline.

Tourmaline is strongly pyroelectric and has been used in depth gauges in submarines. Its electrical properties are remarkable. Tourmaline becomes electric by heat or friction and may be distinguished by this property, which it retains for several hours.

If you find a hatful of tourmaline you'll have an array of gems that will please your eye no matter how plentiful they may be or how inferior to an emerald or ruby in value they continue at the market place. It seems there are about 125 different colors and shades of tourmaline. If you look for it in Georgia, however, you will find only black tourmaline. Those are lustrous enough to be made into black cabochon cuttings. Black stones look lovely in that form. I have a black sapphire I mined that has a double cabochon cut. Black tourmalines in Georgia are generally found in mica mines, granite quarries, and feldspar mines. It is a very popular collector's piece—IF one can search out a velvety black tourmaline.

And here are some spots where you might have good luck and some very pretty tourmaline for your efforts: Riverside, California, and San Diego there; El Paso and Jefferson in Colorado; Litchfield, Connecticut; Middlesex, Connecticut; Androscoggin, Oxford, and Sagadahoc, in Maine; Baltimore, Maryland; Jefferson and Madison in Montana; Cheshire, New Hampshire; Sussex, New Jersey; Orange, New York; Anderson, South Carolina; Custer, South Dakota; Llano, Texas.

Maine is a state where some good gem material in tourmaline is very likely. Only yesterday I saw the most beautiful green tourmaline from that state. It seemed the color of an emerald and as it was embedded in very light matrix it looked deep and vibrant in its rough nest. Besides the spots mentioned above do explore West Paris, Maine. Also Auburn, Minot, Hebron, and penetrate Mount Mica and Norway when you investigate Oxford County. St. Lawrence County, New York, is a tourmaline site, as is Rockingham County in

New Hampshire. In Quebec at Calumet Falls, Pontiac County, you might find some tourmaline too. Check out Argenteuil County in Quebec.

A friend has three tiny hearts made of watermelon tourmaline. The two loops at the top of one heart are green, the center is red and the bottom is white. The three were not identical, of course, with the color distributed differently in each one, but when you consider that this is nature's distribution you must be awed.

If you want to see a gem, a tourmaline of breathtaking beauty, try to track down the pink tourmaline that Cartier fashioned into a marquise shape and cut.

24

❧

Alexandrite and Cat's Eye

Chrysoberyl at Home and Abroad

The gemstone, which was named for Alexander II of Russia, is a variety of chrysoberyl. Some experts have added this, along with the opal, to the list of precious rather than semi-precious gems. Born on the birthday of the Czar and coupling the national colors of red and green, it has always been a Russian favorite—and Russia is where you will most likely find it. However, every friend I know who has a piece of jewelry she calls alexandrite bought it in Egypt. An expert tells me my friends probably bought synthetic sapphire.

This is a gem that is not likely to bore anyone, wearer or viewer. By day, an alexandrite may appear green but in artificial light it becomes a definite raspberry shade. I have just seen one that was huge and there was no other name for it *but* raspberry. However, it does look different to different people and has been called "an emerald by day, an amethyst by night."

Alexandrite differs considerably in appearance from cat's eye and the other chrysoberyl varieties. Chrysoberyl is a mineral that is generally faceted, except for the cat's eye, which contains needlelike inclusions giving it the look of the eye of a cat and is thereby best served by being cut en cabochon.

Chrysoberyl comes from the Greek words—for golden and beryl—but it is definitely not beryl (emerald, aquamarine). It is closer to spinel chemically.

The gemstone alexandrite is one of the newest on the gem

scene, and it is my feeling that both alexandrite and cat's eye will play important parts as fashion stones and enjoy a long reign as stones of intrinsic beauty—and conversation. With so many cat lovers in the country, I am curious as to why this cat's eye stone has not already had an overwhelming success. It is beautiful, mysterious, rare, and quite expensive. Perhaps the idea of that eye following one about is a bit disquieting, and there are those who will tell you it does just that.

The Arabs believed that cat's eye had a property which caused its wearer to become invisible in battle. As an amulet it is supposed to protect a man from witchcraft and death. The most interesting legend about cat's eye, however, is that when a man in Kordofan doubts his wife's fidelity, as he is about to go on a journey he makes her drink milk in which a cat's eye has been washed. The idea is that if after his departure she commits adultery, there will be no children from the union. Amen.

If you have no luck mining cat's eye, there is a marvelous museum-shop on East 34th Street in New York, called Astro Minerals Limited, which has tiger's eye, a hardier-looking stone, but one that looks more like the eye of a tiger than of a cat. You can have a large stone for only $2.50 and one of the smaller ones for $1.50 or $2.00. As I said, it isn't cat's eye but it is the same kind of conversation piece.

I discovered after I began researching alexandrite—shallowly—because there is not that much one can find out about it—that it is one of the gems which makes addicts. I mentioned alexandrite to a gem hound I know and his mouth started to water.

"Ah, there is the stone. There is the treasure. The rarest of stones! It is extremely valuable." I think he thought I had one locked behind my ear because he became silent then as though words had failed him. Unfortunately, unlike my old friend who can whip out almost any gem from his cotton-wrapped packet, I did not have an alexandrite with which to tease the gem hound.

A scattering of chrysoberyl has been found in building excavations in New York. Haddam Neck, in Connecticut, is another place where it may be found and in Boulder County, Colorado. However, the variety of alexandrite my gem hound craved is in Russia, where, incidentally, some of the loveliest gems of history are reposing. There is some alexandrite in Ceylon but like the Russian stones it is found so infrequently a gem hunt to that distant point might be fruitless.

25

❧

Carnelian—A Thirst-quenching Gem

She is a beautiful Persian, and her name is Cleopatra. I was her guest for coffee and she had just finished telling my fortune by turning my coffee cup upside down, finding trees in full bloom and peacocks and other good omens in its demi innards. I felt the star on my shoulder was about to go into orbit taking me with it, so I was in a mood to listen in cat silence as Cleopatra told me a demi legend about carnelian.

It seems people crossing the desert slip a bit of carnelian under their tongue and its moisture keeps them from thirsting. As she talked she fingered a beautiful necklace of carnelian, and since the stones were held together by a ribbon she slipped one off to demonstrate. The stones were quite cool as one felt them.

The carnelian is a stone of ancient heritage and many tales are affixed to it. This quartz gemstone is a clear red-orange chalcedony. The term chalcedony is derived from the name of a town in Asia Minor. Carnelian does not form crystals and when you come upon it in its earthy home it is likely to look more like pieces of broken china than a semi-precious gemstone.

A great number of the Persian and Arab amulets were made from this stone because of the magical power that was believed to exist in it. It was thought that anyone who possessed an amulet in the form of a cylinder seal made of carnelian would never be separated from the protection of his god. The cylinder seal was used as both a seal and an amulet.

Another form of chalcedony has been called "bloodstone." It is hard to believe these are also sisters and part of the quartz kingdom that includes amethyst, rose quartz, etc. However, as an ancient stone, it was alleged to act on the blood and keep it from rising to the head in excess. It was even supposed to stop nosebleeds. A carnelian ring was supposed to make a man slow to anger, render him peaceful. And, here are some promises that will put the entire cosmetic industry on the alert. The carnelian is supposed to make the skin healthy, remove blotches, pimples, and sores. And it is reported that to this day people on the shores of the Mediterranean wear amulets of carnelian to protect them from fascination or the evil eye.

White chalcedony makes a beautiful cameo. And the green "bloodstone" with its flecks of red is lovely, especially when you see it fashioned into tiny pillboxes and decorative snuff boxes, as I have.

Chalcedony artificially stained blue is quite attractive. I once saw a piece done in that way that had been in the collection of Her Majesty, Queen Mary of England. And I have seen a covered box made of carnelian in more natural colors that belonged to Louis XIV. There is a sacrificial knife made of chalcedony in the British Museum. It is fourteenth century Mexican, and melon-colored, and I can't think of anything that looks more lethal and attractive at the same time.

The carnelian is the first stone mentioned in the breastplate of Aaron, and it is presumed it and the other eleven stones were intended to avert every possible evil from the high priest.

Some of the symbolism of the carnelian is that it is a cure for depression. So, if you have moods blacker than pitch start digging for carnelian; it may help to brighten your life. It is also a talisman of friendship.

Chalcedony is so prevalent it can be found in many places: Franklin County, Alabama; Greenlee County, Arizona; San Bernardino County, California, and also Imperial County there; Colorado Springs, El Paso County, Colorado; Somerset

County, New Jersey; Sierra County, New Mexico, also Luna County there; Columbia County, Oregon; Kent County, Rhode Island; Lewiston County, Washington; Johnson County, Wyoming. If you are traveling as far as Nova Scotia you may find some carnelian at Granville Center, Annapolis, County. Lake Superior in Ontario might be explored too. Try Little River, B. C. as well.

The interesting thing about gem hunts is that sometimes when you are searching out one variety of mineral you chance upon another and have a lifetime love affair with it. It could happen with chalcedony and its many varieties.

26

✢

Hawaiian Fantasies

Since it is a bit further than other states and an island group that has its own fairy type of gemstones, Hawaii should have a page of its own.

Pele is the Hawaiian goddess of fire, and delightful ornaments, such as Pele's Tears, Pele's Hair, and Pele's Pearls, are part of her legend. Pele's Tears are quite opaque, glassy black drops broken from the end of filaments of glass drifting away from the fire fountains. Pele's Hair are glass filaments from the action of the fire fountains, but so delicate they tend to disappear. Pele's Pearls, the early ones, were polished gems of hemispherical calcite from cavities in an old quarry. Pele's Pearls have been made from chalcedony from cavities in lavas found near Kailua, Oahu, and from translucent calcite found on Diamond Head.

Then there are Hawaiian "diamonds," cut from calcite at Diamond Head, although some are made from quartz crystals found in the Kailua-Kaneohe area, Oahu.

There are many places to which the Rock Society of Hawaii could lead you. Its Hawaiian name is *Hui Pohaku o Hawaii*. The Bishop Museum in Honolulu has many lovely gems from Oahu and Molokai: gypsum Desert Rose, Hawaiian diamonds, white, green, gray and white, red and gray and brown opal, green moss opal and "eyed" green opal, carnelian, and among dozens of other stones jasper of such shades as yellow, blue, green, blue gray, brown, red, and yellow, and "lizard-skin" jasper. There is also carnelian in matrix, cut olivines, pink agate with chalcedony, pineapple agate, etc.

Hawaiian olivines are the stones which have given substance to the rumor that one walks on peridot in Hawaii as the
sands of the beaches at Diamond Head and Haunama Bay,
Oahu, and South Point, Hawaii, are green with these infini-
tesimal gemstones. You'll find it fun to discover them through
your magnifying glass. Although peridot is rather abundant in
clear stones up to one-eighth carat, olivines sold in Hawaii are
imported from the Southwestern states as the local specimens
are considered too small. Good crystals of olivine can be
collected on the slopes of Puu Io, Puu Keaaliulia, Puu Paapaa,
and Puu Pa on Mauna Kea, Hawaii.

Hawaiian moonstones are banded agate and chalcedony
formerly abundant in the gullies near Olomana Peak, Oahu,
and in the crater of West Molokai.

The black coral found in living "trees" in the deep waters
off Lahaina, Maui, is not fossil coral, of course. It makes
delightful jewelry, and is unique to Hawaii.

If someone mentions Hawaiian topaz, he is probably talking about the so-called Hawaiian sunstones cut from yellow
crystals of plagioclase feldspar, so plentiful on the cinder cone
at Manele Bay, Lanai, or Pohakea Pass, Oahu.

The world of delicious gems in Hawaii goes on and on.
This is a holiday spot where you not only swim in aquamarine
water but you walk on peridot as well. With such treasure
lurking it would seem any and all of us have a lovely excuse to
fly or sail the Pacific.

27

✤

Surface Mining and Treasure Trove Half-hints

If you do not surface mine where gemstones have already been discovered you need more than your share of lady luck, although a basic knowledge of geology will give you a head start even as a pioneer in gems. Whether you go into areas already discovered, and those areas are teeming with gems or only sprinkled with them, or you decide to go out on your own and hunt new gem grounds, here are some hints that may be helpful to you.

1. Track down a geologic map that will tell you WHICH gemstones you are likely to find by surface mining.

2. Find out WHERE the specific deposits are of the particular gems in which you are interested. A good start would be to write for the latest Geological Survey Bulletin on gemstones. Request this of the Superintendent of Documents, U.S. Government Printing Office, Washington, D.C. Be certain to enclose twenty-five cents for the bulletin and specify "gemstones" or you may get a bulletin dealing with other rocks or minerals.

3. In any state or locality where you might wish additional information there are many outlets you can contact, since from state to state department names differ. Museums within a state and state universities are very helpful. They nearly always have good geologic ties and can put you in immediate touch with what you need even if they cannot supply it. They are invaluable in recommending reading material on mining or "collecting" as they are more likely to call it. Also, geologic societies within the state can be helpful. Needless to say, the

state Chamber of Commerce will give you good leads—so start with your own state if it appears to be gem-studded.

4. Study carefully the rock types so you will not only know which ones reach the surface or near it but also HOW you can identify what you are searching for in each specific gem area. Don't try to become an authority on the entire gem world overnight. Take the stones one at a time and study each one assiduously. However, you *will* find that digging at a particular place for, let us say, corundum (ruby and sapphire) may turn up a rhodolite garnet. So while it is good to know the stone you are interested in very thoroughly, it is wise to have, at least, a surface knowledge of some of the other stones you are likely to encounter in the same mineral situation.

5. Surface mining requires tools in some spots and no tools in others. As mentioned, when we went ruby and sapphire hunting we took nothing but our own toil with us, but I wish now I had been foresighted enough to take my magnifying glass as there are many stones I now know and I could have missed them in my quest for rubies and sapphires. The magnifying glass might have pointed up some features I could have pursued. A glass tells tales no other handy instrument is likely to reveal so quickly. You might end up as your own gemologist.

Our ruby and sapphire mining was very civilized indeed, if a bit sooty. We stood at table frames with sieve bottom boxes and hosed down the soil in the box trays. At Gibson's we let the running water wash over our trays and through the gem gravel as we agitated it. This is the same idea as the Holbrook hosing operation—washing the soil away until the heavier stones are left and then sorting out the gems from the gravel. You can see where no tools of any kind are necessary here.

However, for amethyst, emerald, quartz generally, opal, and many other stones, picks, sledge hammers, or geologic hammers are recommended. Here is a complete list of things you may find helpful, although you will not use all of them at any one time. At one place, for instance, you might use just a small spade to tumble the earth a bit to find fresh material. In any event, depending on how seriously you plan to pursue your gemstones surface mining career, here is a long, perhaps, but easy to handle list of possibles.

1 • A FIELD BAG of some kind with a shoulder strap so you can keep it as far or near to you as you wish.

2 • A MAGNIFYING GLASS, as maximum as you can afford.

3 • A PICK OR A PENKNIFE.

4 • A NOTEBOOK and two good sharp pencils. You will want to identify stones from particular areas and take other notes, so be prepared for "jottings."

5 • A GEOLOGICAL OR A SLEDGE HAMMER. Be careful how you use this when removing a specimen. Always aim the striking blow away from the gem material, reducing the rock around it a very small piece at a time. The crystallized minerals are the most difficult of all to obtain because the danger of destroying them is so great. If the mineral gem you are after is deeply embedded in rock it can be removed by cutting a deep trench around it with a chisel. The great horror in finding a perfect gemstone embedded in difficult surroundings is to know that unless you take time and care the treasure will become worthless through *your* lack of talent and not through nature's.

6 • A COLD CHISEL is a good investment as the above will attest. Get one about five inches long with a cutting edge of a half inch.

7 • A CHEAP HEAVY PAIR OF GLOVES. Although our mining was gloveless, I did try to save my manicure a few times, but it interfered with my speed and rhythm and finally I had to discard the little cotton gloves I tried to wear when agitating the stones. However, as the chapter on amethysts and quartz will tell you, good heavy gloves are a "must" in many mining situations. And you may find yourself visiting the local five and dime store for a second pair before your mining expedition is behind you.

8 • A SMALL SPADE. Dig you must at one time or another

so it is good to have a spade with you when you know you will do your own digging far from any place where you can borrow one. The people who personally dug their own treasure at Holbrook's were given spades that were lying about in the pit for their use.

9 • GOGGLES. Not just sunglasses, but glasses that will protect your eyes completely. Chipping rocks is precarious, especially when you become so absorbed and bend over the specimens to unearth them. Do protect yourself with these. I remember my own eye-to-eye status with the rubies and sapphires I hosed down and even then I received an eyeful of water many times. The likelihood of flying quartz or rock chips is very high.

10 • A COMPASS. You just might want to carry one of these, especially if you are adventure prone.

11 • NEWSPAPER OR CLOTH. Bring some kind of paper or cloth with you in which to wrap larger specimens. However, if you are gem hunting only, as we were, you might want to carry the preserve jar or pill bottles. We found the little plastic pill bottles were very handy as you could put them in your pocket while you were mining and just drop in the specimens as you found them.

THIS IS A FAIRLY COMPLETE LIST OF THINGS YOU ARE LIKELY TO NEED—NOT INCLUDING MAPS AND OTHER TIDY CARRYALLS— FOR SURFACE MINING IN ANY EMERGENCY SHORT OF THE HILLS BURYING YOU OVER.

Surface mining is exactly what the term would indicate, deposits that are close to or on the surface. This, for our purposes, would mean open pit mining and alluvial mining.

Open pit mining requires frequent bulldozing or plowing to unearth fresh material but the owners of the gem fields that are open to the public take care of that and see that the gem mines are "lively" most of the time.

Alluvial mining is performed in sand and gravel deposits where various mineral specimens contain gemstones. Diamonds may be sought in the placer deposits. (These are the mineral deposits in stream beds.) The hardier stones are concentrated there as they are able to withstand the rubbing and buffeting of the lighter materials which are carried away or pulverized eventually. Since the diamonds are the hardiest of stones—and weighty—they are a natural deposit and might be picked or panned in stream beds. The Great Lakes areas are spots where great diamond "find" possibilities lie. If you are alluvial mining for diamonds you can do it with great optimism in that area of the country.

The technique of panning is simple, exactly as it is for gold. A location is marked out and the miner scoops the soil and gravel, which he hopes is gem bearing, into his washbasin-type pan. Gem materials, being heavier, will not stay above the soil, and as the soil is eliminated through agitation and being mixed with water the gemstones are recognized. The best miners' pan, to my mind, is a sieve-bottom one, finely meshed, so that the water can be juggled through it easily and the unwanted soil can escape in a quick liquid stream to reveal the gem goodies. Of course in gold panning, when each tiny flake counts, the sieve bottom pan is not as practical as the closed bottom pan. As one continues to mine he will find newer and simpler ways to hunt his treasure. And so you will remember how close the treasure might be to you I'll say here the treasured, world-valuable emerald is a mineral of the old, deep rocks which have been exposed by weathering—surfaced for the taking by you. How about starting your gem hunt with a trip to Alexander County in North Carolina where, I am told, you *could* find an e——d!

It seems mundane to mention it, but you must wear comfortable clothing when you mine. You may think my story of the dry cleaner's bag was an exaggeration, but once the water started to splash and the soil began to fly I was deeply grateful for the ingenuity of my friends, who had wrapped me in cellophane. Low-heeled sturdy shoes are a must. Loafers are a good suggestion. I wore gum-soled moccasins. They keep out soil and what dampness you will encounter. If you are female, wear something on your head. Somehow hair turns loose during the excitement of mining and all of a sudden the golliwogs are neater-headed than you are. Also, if you are mining in the sun, the top of your head can feel like a fried egg quite soon—not to mention the scrambled variety of your brain inside.

Keep cool—and patience will help you toward *that*. This is an admonition to be taken both literally and figuratively. Although surface mining can be more fun than anything you have ever done, it can also be long, hot, and somewhat nerve-wracking if the circumstances dictate the script that way. I'm thinking of you taking a wrong turn in the road, ending up in the wrong spot, and digging until blisters show without a shadow of hope for even a jumping bean for all your trouble. And it happens.

Always know where you are going, what you may find when you get there, what, approximately, it looks like, how you will identify it when you meet it, and how to get it as carefully, if not speedily, as possible.

28

❧

What to Do with Your Treasures!

Each of us feels differently about his gem discoveries. The first step, of course, is to find out what the gemstone is worth. Usually the mining area has several gemologists and the mine owner will surely be able to refer you to a competent man.

When you know for sure that the stone is worth cutting and polishing you can make the decision as to how it might be done. There, too, the gemologist is helpful. He will be able to tell you whether the stone will lend itself more fittingly to the *brilliant* cut with its fifty-eight facets—the *step brilliant* has seventy-eight facets—or whether the star lurking in its asteriated beauty will shine brighter through a *cabochon* or domed cut. The *step or trap cut* is also called the *emerald cut*, as it exposes the COLOR of a gem through its large table. Since you are likely to find stones that will lend themselves to this cut, popularly called *the emerald cut*, we might dwell a bit on it. It has a flat table, either oblong or square. This cut undoubtedly grew out of two things. The great beauty of the emerald *color* is set off by this cutting, which accentuates shade, and the difficulty in faceting due to the loss of gem material is reduced. For the latter reason emeralds are very frequently cut en cabochon. Faceted emeralds are so beautiful, however, they literally take your breath away. I saw a group of them recently and I am still gasping. Apparently, no matter what you do to an emerald it still talks to you from its "deeps." Besides the emerald, there are so many other gorgeous stones whose shades cry out to be seen and the so-called "emerald cut" is a popular answer. However, cushion antique is considered THE cut for faceted rubies and sapphires.

The *rose* cut was popular with the Victorians, perhaps because it is so delightful for smaller diamonds, and it might be a good cut for making some of those "teenies" you will mine look great grouped with a real or cultured pearl. This cutting is one of twenty-four facets, with the division of six star facets known as the crown and eighteen facets known as the dentelle. When the underpart is a repetition of the upper it is called *double rose*. As someone has said, "It looks like a gumdrop." It does. The *cabochon* may be treated in much the same way. Although the simple cabochon has a flat base, the *double cabochon* is a duplicate of the dome on the bottom as well as on the top. My black sapphire was cut in this double cabochon manner and it is quite intriguing.

While these are the basic forms of cutting—the brilliant, the step, trap, or emerald cut, the cabochon, and the rose— there are many other forms and one's ingenuity is always adding more. The *marquise*, the *pendeloque*, the *baguette*, are some of those. The *marquise* shape is like a pointed oval. The pair of yellow diamonds in Tillie Lewis's beautiful breakfast brooch are cut in this manner. They could not be more beautiful, as the fifty-eight facets expose the matchless fire of the diamond brilliant. The *pendeloque* enjoys great modern popularity in its pear-shaped blaze. The *baguette* is a thin vertical cutting, frequently used with stones of other faceting. Allow yourself to be influenced by the gemologist. He will know better than you, initially, what cutting your stone needs.

After you have your gems cut and polished, what then? You think you will want to transfer them to jewelry settings immediately but that isn't how it happens. They are yours—you mined them—and you want to view them as they are as long as you can. So, if you are the ordinary, garden variety of collector you will find a Riker Mount (that shallow cardboard box with a glass lid) and you will put your gems in that on a bed of cotton until you can think out exactly what you want to do with them, and of course you'll offer a view of them to friends and deadly foes alike.

It is wise to put your gems into the hands of the best lapidary or gemologist possible, but don't disallow your own creativity. Here are some charming (*j'espère*) "now and then" ideas of what you can do with rings, pins, lockets, necklaces, bracelets, and more. Also, I think one of the most chic things you might do is have the stones put in a set of drinking goblets—silver, if possible—whether they be for water or any other libation. Imagine the conversation going something like this as you entertain old friends:

"My, what a handsome goblet. That's a mighty pretty red stone."

"Oh," offhandedly, "the ruby? Yes, it's quite a good one."

"Ruby?" Guest takes a quick swag of contents of cup. "A real ruby?"

"Just one I mined, but it IS three carats and quite pure." Guest empties rest of goblet and sets it on the table as though it were the Holy Grail. Has nothing more to say at the moment. A screech across the room involves everyone again.

"Do you mean to say I am drinking from a cup with a real amethyst in it?" your best friend, who always knew you kept things from her, accuses.

"Oh, amethysts are only semi-precious stones, you know," you instruct her, not realizing all ties of friendship have temporarily been broken. She puts down goblet resolving to tell you NOTHING in the future. By the time the garnet, topaz, and maybe even an eensy tweensy diamond are discovered you realize you may have lost all your friends but your party is the smash of the season. The clamor for information about your jewel-encrusted drinking vessels will overcome all other feelings or motives and you will be able to talk for months without getting to the bottom of your mining adventures or to the end of the tales of your gem finds. By that time you may be running for senator or maybe only councilman but for a lovely moment in history you were surely up there with the speakers and the spoken about.

If you have small stones you might like putting them around a silver or gold picture frame. They are exquisite on miniature frames. I have collected portrait miniatures for many years and the frames of the pictures have become as cherished as the miniatures themselves, although I am not likely to turn away from a Nicholas Hilliard or a Samuel Cooper portrait in favor of a bad painting with an amethyst, topaz, or diamond of great beauty.

RINGS lend themselves to so many ideas. There are betrothal rings, signet rings, watch rings, mourning rings, coronation rings, portrait rings, lovers rings, poison rings, gimmal rings, astrological rings, and so many others. You can guide any jeweler of talent to make the ring of your choice. Here are what some rings might look like, translated from antiquity.

THE POISON RING can be one of the most attractive. I stumbled on one in London many years ago and it is one of my most cherished possessions. It is sometimes called the Borgia Ring. Mine is, like many poison rings, a circlet that opens like a small safe on a spring. It has a rather large amethyst in the center and several small amethysts clustered around the base below the center jewel of the cover. This type of poison ring was a bit nicer than some others. It once held a tiny pellet, perhaps to slip into someone's drink or to do oneself in if life and limb at the moment seemed particularly dark. Today, you can slip a tiny wad of cotton saturated with your favorite scent into the opening—and every man near you will want to nibble on your finger. The other poison rings had a more sinister note and shaking hands with someone who wore one became more *"adios"* than *"buenos días."* These rings had pointed ends which were slipped from the back of the hand to the palm and when a murderer wished to eliminate an enemy he pressed the poison-filled points into the other man's hand with a fearful squeeze. I have never been able to understand how he was himself totally protected. I am sure there were some strange backfirings in that unfriendly gesture, the squeeze.

VISIBILITY RINGS were provocative creations. As mentioned earlier, the carbuncle was alleged to glow in the dark and a ring set with this stone was supposed TO MAKE ONE VISIBLE IN THE DEEPEST PIT. Well, if Noah lighted his ark with it, how can we quarrel with the idea? *I* am interested in the legendary *in*visibility rings. I can't tell you how they are created, but I wish I knew. I wish I knew!

Among the LOVERS RINGS of the Middle Ages were the *gimmal rings*. These were two circlets fitted into each other, separated and given one to each partner at the betrothal, then joined together at the wedding.

What we must remember about rings of the Middle Ages and later—the wearers did not stop with one—or even with one on every finger. Hands literally dripped with rings, and any visit to a museum will confirm this if you examine the jewelry of royal subjects in paintings. I have worn five to six rings on my small finger for years, but a visit to the tomb of Juan of Austria, considered the handsomest man in the world, led me into still further fashion excesses with rings. Juan, whose sarcophagus has to be the most beautiful piece of marble in existence, wears rings above and below the knuckles of both his hands. I am sure many of my ruby finds will end as finger jewelry, but what better way to be found if one loses her way in the dark.

WATCH RINGS are delightful, and you will find these around. However, a watch ring with a cover studded with a beautiful stone is a thing of double beauty. And, if you want to make it really a conversation piece, you can make it a three-way ring by putting the watch on a spring hinge that opens to a pillbox underneath. The watch ring would not have to be very wide but it could be high and handsome.

ASTROLOGICAL RINGS with signs of the zodiac represented in one way or the other are a great favorite, especially since astrology is enjoying an incredible popularity at the moment. Your sign and your stone—a delightful idea that is drenched in tradition.

RELIGIOUS RINGS can be glorious. Remember the beautiful

amethyst rings of Roman Catholic bishops. The religious rings can be inscribed with foreign language proverbs *"Sin Mi nada podeis hacer* (Without Me you can do nothing) or some French or Latin motto of your choice. One ring of the tenth to eleventh century I saw was Byzantine and shows the importance of punctuation. Silver, it is inscribed: "Lord, help the wearer."

In spite of their somewhat somber beginnings MOURNING RINGS can be made into exquisite memorials. Sometimes the picture or portrait of the lost one is on the face of the ring and a lock of his or her hair is in the back of it under glass. Many of these are reversible or have tiny chambers that open with a spring catch like the poison rings, in which the hair lock, usually braided, is kept.

If you are one of those who must have a hand in everything, you will want to create your WEDDING RING from the idea right onto your hand. This is a ring that should have no restrictions. Unless you want to have "his" and "hers" wedding rings, go the limit and make your wedding ring as lovely as any ring has a right to be. Pour into its thought all the warmth and beauty and feeling that you have for your bridal partner. Stud it with stones or follow the idea of having both of your initials in tiny chips.

It should be mentioned that in antiquity the right hand rather than the currently popular left hand was the repository of the wedding ring, and it was usually worn on the middle joint of the fourth finger. The middle joint of the finger was a common ring bearer, in any event. I am convinced that the world was peopled, in those days, only by those with so-called philosopher's fingers. How else could those rings have stayed on? Of course, the same little hands seldom knew any activity except to flutter a fan, but it would seem likely that the little dears waved "good-by" or something strenuous sometimes.

TALISMAN RINGS are delights—and each of us has a favorite saying that might make a good daily reminder if it were inscribed in or on the ring too.

LOVERS RINGS should make us more creative than anything

else. A single pearl matched by a literary gem in verse, perhaps. Dot all the i's of a loving tribute with tiny diamonds
and don't think she won't make that her most cherished piece
of jewelry. The possibilities are enormous and only you can
put an end or limit to what can be done with gemstones in a
lover's ring.

Considering the masses of lovers the world is producing
today, and the volumes of words they are expelling about their
feelings, it would seem to be the perfect time to concentrate
on lovers' rings but there is another kind of ring which could
outrank it in popularity, similar to it, it is called the POSY
RING. The "posy" does not mean a flower but rather the
"poesy" of verse. So any ring which has a saying or verse of a
love-locked nature is properly a posy ring, but it would also
seem to be interchangeable with the lovers ring.

The love rings from medieval times were very creative, and
right through the centuries they were charming. The Victoria
and Albert Museum in London has many and two, particularly, come to mind. English and eighteenth century, one says,
"IT SHAKES A STEADY MIND" and the other, "STOP THIEF."

Then there is the fourteenth century silver ring that says
"AMOUR MERCI."

The fifteenth century charm of
"VOUS ET NUL AUTRE."

And from 1400, English, a lovely amethyst with the inscription
"PAR GRANT AMOUR."

A silver gilt, fifteenth century ring says
"C'EST MON PLESIR."

One of the FEDE (friendship) RINGS I particularly liked was
the laconic, fifteenth century, silver gilt one that tossed off
"BINDIT AS FINDIT."

Gold, fifteenth century English rings wooed their loves with
French phrases, for four more say
"DE BON COEUR."

"PENSE DE MOY."

"A TANT OUBLIE"
"POUR TOUJOURS."

There was a touching signet ring of gold, 1450, English, which said, "EDMUND, TOUT MA VIE." One could almost know Edmund never removed that ring.

If those don't inspire you how about these centuries-old lovers-posy ring inscriptions:

"All I refuse and thee I choose."
"If love you bear this for me wear."
"In love linkt fast while life doth last."
"As dear to me as life can be."

But one of the oldest ring customs is one I discovered in the Caledonian Market in London where I found an old MIZPAH RING in that well-known flea market. The Mizpah (which comes from Hebrew and means "a place for keeping a lookout or watch") has one of the most touching inscriptions of antiquity, right for any age, especially for a wedding ring: "The Lord watch between me and thee when we are absent one from the other." The Mizpah may also be a pin, as I had a silver pin with the inscription. When you have a very little stone you might want to put it in a Mizpah ring or pin to brighten its look. Its sentiment needs no coddling.

PORTRAIT RINGS are beautiful, and can be colored photographs, portraits, or black and white photos retouched. I have an old miniature ring, a portrait of a Georgian gentleman. It is quite large—for a ring—but very lovely and one day I shall have it framed to join my collection of portrait miniatures. Portrait rings make good lovers rings. Give him a portrait of you set in a ring and have him give you a portrait of himself done in the same way, perhaps to match the setting. It makes a conversation piece, gives you a chance to talk about the love of your life, and in this age of hip-hoppie jewelry it would be a welcome ornament.

Then, there are the SEAL RINGS, and if you are lucky, perhaps like Solomon's was alleged to do, you may find yours works "magic" too. Solomon, the King, was known as a magician, according to legend. His ring, with which he was said to work miracles, was of pure gold and set with a single stone, usually thought to have been a diamond. The ineffable name of God, YHWH, was considered the source of power for the magic and was engraved on the ring. The stones *you* will find will suggest little magics of their own.

In the Mineral Department of the British Museum of. Natural History I saw an ARCHER'S THUMB RING. That would seem to be a good place to end the conversation on rings, for what more exotic place is there to put a ring than on your thumb!

We seem to have concentrated in depth on the categories of rings you can make from your stone but here are a few other ideas.

TIE PINS OR SCARF PINS. These are delightful for so many purposes, including wearing as you would a brooch. I use tie pins on just about every costume I own that has a collar.

TIE TACK. Make your Christmas booty just that . . . a tie tack for HIM with a gem you mined.

After rings BRACELETS lend themselves to the most possibilities because multi-colored stones look so lovely in creative bracelet settings. I can never forget the beauty of those lovely pale sapphires—so many hues of the stone—sparkling elegantly from their delicate framework.

There are some ideas for pious jewelry. I thought of these after reading about the 99 BEAD ROSARY OF THE ARABS. Each bead is associated with one of the names of Allah, and the one hundredth item of the rosary is a pillar reserved for the name of God. Since many of the Arab rosaries were made from agates you might like to search out that area of the mineral world for a stone to pursue, and a good reason for pursuing it.

If you have a good Catholic rosary you might like to substitute a ruby or sapphire find for each gloria or do an entire rosary of small stones. It would be a sure way of sending you to your knees, and give you an out-of-this-world excuse for fingering your treasure daily.

You might have the stones of your quest, if it is very successful, put into a Buddhist rosary containing 100 or 108 beads. It is worn like a necklace or wrapped around the wrist like a bracelet.

Or you might have your gemstones made into tiny lights on a gold cross.

A bright colored stone in each corner of the hexagram might make a lovely pendant or charm for a Judaic friend or three.

Do you love your spouse or only think you do? Maria Theresia, that fascinating Empress of eighteenth century Austria, proved her affection by presenting her husband, who was a collector of precious stones, with a bouquet of the most beautiful precious and semi-precious stones one could imagine. I saw it—emeralds, rubies, opals, sapphires, topaz, turquoise, and garnets in the nineteen-and-one-half-inch-high gem-studded posy. With an extravagant mother like that how could her daughter, Marie Antoinette, expect the citizens of France to eat anything else but cake?

The artisans of the fifteenth and sixteenth centuries, as one looks at their works, remind us that they took the same pains to create a bracelet as an artist did to paint a treasure for tomorrow. A pear-wood model of a sixteenth century carved bracelet by Hans Kels the Elder overwhelms one with its integrity of detail. What an admonition their talent is to today's planned obsolescence!

Why not create something out of your gemstones that your children or your heirs will cherish long into the future? Even if you think your stone is minor, the proper setting can make it seem quite important.

NECKLACES are another gem wonder. If you have no ideas at all for a necklace, make the largest gem you have into a clasp for your favorite natural or cultured pearls. Necklaces assumed enormous popularity when necklines began to drop. No matter how beautiful a woman's neck or throat may be, the addition of beautiful gems will enhance it. A beautiful gold chain with a single, gloriously set ruby—perhaps surrounded by tiny diamonds—could be staggering. A pair of sapphires tied in a single twin setting like a lover's bow is a thought. Imagine an emerald as a clasp on pink pearls!

The possibilities for gem settings are enough to make one's head swim. It is important to FIND the stones. There is something else you can do with your "finds"—*you can set styles with them.* If you have your best stone set in a ring, set it in one of those perfume rings we spoke about. They have the same look as the old poison rings—that little chamber on springs—but instead of holding poison, either powder or pellet, use a different perfume for each occasion. Change the little cotton tuft as often as you change your mood. If the chamber is filigree there is a better chance for the aroma to escape and anyone who gets near your hand will want to keep it and not just for the jewel it carries.

If you find many small stones—and finds run like that— have them cut just right for their kind and set them in or around a large double-faced locket, an open one. Put a picture of your favorite person in it, changing it when you need to. You'll create quite a bit of conversation, and people will practically line up to see who the man of THAT hour is.

One of the areas of the home that is so dressed up these days is the bathroom. Why not bejewel the ornament drinking glass that no one can miss? . . . And if you really want the world to know you have found a ruby, wear it right in the middle of your forehead. It might have been done before, but on you it will have the additional charm of being a beacon and lead you out of dark places—or at least more or less guarantee you will be found.

Now that rings are so very much in fashion and people are wearing them in singles and doubles on every finger, we might introduce the GAME OF RING SPEECH. The way and the quantity of rings worn have their own message.

Wearing just one ring—Independent you are, but perhaps a bit lonely.

Wearing two rings—both on the same finger—You are in love and won't be separated from the lover.

Wearing three rings on one hand, not necessarily on one finger—Means you are a bit fickle.

Wearing four rings on one hand—Means you are very popular and very fickle.

Wearing five rings, especially if one is large and dominates your index finger—Means you are a femme fatale.

Wearing rings on both hands—Means you are too dressed up to wear any other jewelry—so never, never slip a bracelet on your arm while you are playing the double ring game.

Wearing a man's ring, on any finger—Means you have powerful charms to have gotten it away from him. If he wears yours—it can only mean he has a very little, little finger or can be talked into anything.

Each of us has a dream of possession. One of us wants to own a gold-plated Rolls Royce, another a house with yellow shutters, and there are those of us who would care deeply for a lamp that honors wishes. But my dream of dreams is a piece of jewelry made for Maximilian III Joseph in the eighteenth century. It is a Golden Fleece, and of all the jewelry of history dedicated to orders of one kind or another this is the loveliest in my estimation. It is made of pink and white brilliants in an exquisite gold setting. Apparently I am destined to admire the taste of that gentleman because a second Order of the Golden Fleece made for the Bavarian Elector contains the Whittelsbach blue diamond surrounded by white diamonds and it is nearly as dazzling. It was made earlier than the pink and white enchantment, however.

29

A Stone for Everyone!

To know the birthstones for every month of the year might send you in search of your natal stone.

JANUARY—the *garnet*. Try to find the beautiful rhodolite, which can be achingly lovely.

FEBRUARY—the *amethyst*. If you wish to be wined, but not headless, this is your talisman.

MARCH—the *aquamarine*. That sea-colored beryl so much less costly than its sister beryl, the emerald, but pastel lovely as it swims in its own marine colors.

APRIL—the *diamond*. A cool poem of gemology. There will never be a last word on this gem.

MAY—the *emerald*. Tantalizing with its double personality of fiery depths and cool cover. An enigma, and an eye ease.

JUNE—the *pearl*. Pure and fragile. A timeless beauty in any setting.

JULY—the *ruby*. That fiery lamp. The sun stone. A rajah's reward. The gem of blazing beauty.

AUGUST—the *sardonyx*—and *the peridot*, that discriminating blaze of green-gold.

SEPTEMBER—the *sapphire*. Cool blue. Untiring beauty and talisman of wit and wisdom.

OCTOBER—the *opal*. Creamy or darkly beautiful. A good luck charm if it is your stone.

NOVEMBER—the *topaz*. Golden beauty that glows as blue or pink beauty—and more.

DECEMBER—the *turquoise*. That Persian favorite—and *lapis lazuli*, the rock gem as ancient as Egypt.

Try to know not only your own stone but the stones of your friends. Nothing would please more as a gift than a birthstone you mined and had set for someone you are fond of. I had some of my tiniest stones—rubies and sapphires in the rough —placed under a cabochon-shaped, magnifying, paperweight dome for a friend and he was almost beside himself with delight that I had gone to such creative lengths to please him.

While it is true the lapidary or gemologist can ruin or rarefy your gemstone, the setting of your stone must be in equally competent hands. That means that if you have found a good-sized ruby or even a small, nearly perfect one, don't do something foolish like having it set in pinchbeck or an inferior metal. Make its frame worthy of the perfection of the stone. A beautiful gold setting is relatively inexpensive and lasting.

Something that is very beautiful and not too often seen these days is lovely enameled jewelry. Enameling on jewelry is actually glass. Dorothy Dignam told me about a rough diamond she bought for three dollars and had made into an exquisite piece of jewelry, a ring, by having it put into an enameled setting.

It is amazing how important jewelry has been through the ages. Even an artist like Titian painted his nudes with earrings and necklaces as though he did not believe a thing of perfect creation like the human body could be perfectly beautiful without the addition of another kind of jewel.

There is a strange thing about a jewel and a jeweler. Jewelers are artists in their own field and if a person is a non-personality it is an inhibiting factor when the jeweler attempts to create for the real "who?"

Men have this quality as well as women. Have you ever noticed how gracefully royalty wears his jewels, regardless of how much man, solid and incontestable, is stored up in his person? That is because gemstones are part of his heritage and he is wearing a visible part of his background. Some men in apparently humble surroundings have this quality. Maybe that is what is meant by "sleeping princes." Conversely, some people of title have looked as though they were wearing broken windowpanes instead of a treasury in jewels.

A jeweler is quick to know what is right for you, so if you mine sapphires and rubies and he recommends the sapphires for you, follow his advice. Then, they will be right for you, for your skin tones, your personality—and they will serve you as the ruby might serve a relative for whom you could have it set.

Jewelry is more a part of twentieth century living than it has been of any other century because almost everyone owns some piece of jewelry, and ornament belongs to any hour of the day. I agree with the Queen of England, who never looked so regal as when she wore a beautiful diamond and emerald brooch fastened to the lapel of her tweeds, as she snipped the tape at a day nursery.

30

❧

Some Loud Thinking About Gems and Gemstones

If you have never felt any emotion for a gemstone, there may be something in your soul to be awakened. Following gems has led me into glittering fields that admonished me as a poet for not having found them before.

Soon after my own awareness, I wanted to know how other people felt about gems. I began, you will never guess where—with a clergyman! I felt he was certain to be the most objective, since the monetary value of gemstones would not be his reason for defending or defeating them.

An English Jesuit, Joseph Christie, S.J., gave me some of the most articulate, thoughtful musings I was able to gather on the subject.

"How do I feel about a diamond?" he repeated. "I find beauty, but I find coldness and hardness in it. I find a cleverness that could be painful." A good beginning, I thought. Some of our award-winning movies don't leave that many impressions with us.

When I asked Father Christie about the pearl—the precious pearl—he became more relaxed and even more expansive, and he mixed his feelings with those of another famous preacher, Ronald Knox. "The pearl is the emblem of creation and the development of thought. There is the old oyster sitting in his shell, waiting to be eaten. A parasite bores its way through and the oyster produces a pearl—like a man having a great thought. The friction that produces the pearl could be considered the opposition to the man's thought. In the cultured pearl, the inserted plague creates the gem. How much does our culture depend on opposition."

His ideas on the emerald were less optimistic. "The emerald is always associated with misfortune, isn't it?" he said, obviously associating it with some personal misadventure as so many people do with so many things, however unconsciously. I can't agree with the idea of the emerald being a misfortune stone, especially as it has been called "the lovers stone," as I reminded him. And since it is the most costly of all gems today, it is a good fortune stone just in view of its market value.

When one reads the history of gems and knows the care and affection that have been lavished on a gem of great renown it is like coming across an old friend or a royal guest when she finally sees a gem of the ages.

One of the most daring and nearly perfect gem robberies of modern times was the theft of the De Long Ruby, the Star of India Sapphire, and other treasure spirited from the vaulted Museum of Natural History in New York. One wonders, though, what really impelled the daring thieves to steal the gem treasures. Many other, less difficult to secure accesses to money must have presented themselves to the men. Perhaps it was the daring execution of the theft, the Raffles instinct to see if it could be done. Perhaps it was the beauty of the jewels that was irresistible. Whatever the reason, the mystery, the outrageous deed, had a flavor of medieval derring-do, a quality or risking much for much. Money is only money, they seemed to say, but if you must make off with treasure, let it be something that shines like the eyes of an ancient idol or sprays stars with dazzling brilliance.

It would seem that one could almost FEEL a paste diamond or other imitation gemstone, but sophisticated people, very worldly people, have worn imitation jewels for years without knowing they had been swindled or that an ancestor had been less than inquiring into the history of the family gem he left to his heirs. A test with a file readily separates paste stones from nature's own gemstones. Any glass will yield to this scratch test. Paste diamonds may fool you, but they are composed of ordinary crown glass or flint glass; it is a dense lead flint glass of high refraction and very strong color dispersion.

When a roguish dealer wishes to outsmart even a keen customer who is shopping for a good *shade* of stone and also wishes to meet the tests of hardness, an ingenious two part stone is conceived. The top is, perhaps, very pale or badly colored. The bottom is the right, darker shade or whatever the requisite tinge or hue is—but it is an imitation stone. This pairing is called a doublet. The simulated stone of right shading shows through to the top and appears to be the same color throughout. A device called the triplet has been devised in case the base should also be tested for hardness. This is a sandwich type of stone—colorless stones form top and bottom and colored cement in the middle gives the desired shade. The imitation band is hidden by the setting. It seems like a lot of work to be reprehensible, but it does succeed in making a pale gemstone look more vital. There would seem to be more reasons to mine one's own stones than just the fun and economy of mining. There are many ways to be overwhelmed in buying jewelry, and since it is an expensive item on anyone's budget one should know the stones she buys as well as the meat and vegetables she selects.

When you remember that the present market price of diamonds runs from as low as seventy-five dollars for one-quarter of a carat to seven thousand dollars for a superior two-carat stone, it behooves anyone to know what she is buying and from whom she is buying it.

People have a tendency to buy semi-precious and precious stones when they travel. There's something about seeing a gem in a foreign setting that makes it twice as important to us. But the buyer must be more careful. Since there is a natural progression from gem mining to gem buying, especially rough stones, and you will even find yourself swapping stones, as a collector, you should study the pitfalls as well as the glories of the hobby.

Verneuil invented the inverted blowpipe to manufacture synthetic rubies that defied easy detection. I might say this blowpipe looked more like a Rube Goldberg invention than what it was intended to be, but it worked perfectly. Under the proper tests, however, the artificial stones almost always showed tiny air bubbles and did not have the straight striations (fine lines) of the natural ruby. There is always something to give away an imitation.

31

❧

A Gem-splashed Holiday for the Whole Family

Every year, families all over the country, count their box tops or whatever will see them through at least a two-week holiday, and dream of the hour and the minute they can take off for fun and games. But most of us tend to make even a trip to the beach more of a pedestrian outing than it needs to be.

Make a promise to yourself this year. Tell YOURSELF that you are leaving behind, on your next holiday, every possible worry or workday wrinkle. Imagine the gleam you will put into the eyes of that married-to-you-for-seven-years wife one dazzling day as you lean down to say, "I'm going to find you the largest ruby in the Cowee Valley, honey!" After she realizes you haven't taken up illegal entry as a Sunday hobby she'll add her head to yours and you can plan one of the real adventures of your family life.

Children are especially enchanted with the idea of gem mining or rock mining of any description so they will be your natural allies in any plans. Here's a chronology that should work out to be one hundred percent fun. Write your wife a letter, as one of her Christmas presents, inviting her to escape with you and the children to the cool comforts of the Blue Ridge Mountains for a spree of gems, come summer—or whenever you are sprung from your personal work cage.

As part of her Christmas "loot" give her a map of the locality you plan to cover and fill a Christmas stocking for her with all the smaller items she is likely to use on the trip—the magnifying glass, pencils, pad, pick, hammer, goggles, and whatever else you think will fit into the stocking. Or—slip everything into a handsome field bag as one of her major presents. Make sure it has a shoulder strap. No wife who has the promise of a jarful of gems will be anything but pleased at the idea of going on such a picnic. Do the same thing for the children. If each one has his own map or gear he will feel more important and will become quite self-sufficient on the safari. One of the good things about such an expedition is that it is such a consuming occupation for children it keeps them interested beyond any parent's hopes. There is always something they will want to prepare, and you can send them to the library to look up more information about the stones they are interested in. They will even become museum addicts since so many museums have gem and rock collections that will fascinate them. When you are ready to start your holiday don't be too surprised if the children know more about the vacation surprise you have for them than you do.

You don't have to go far from your own home to find gemstones as they may be found IN EVERY ONE OF THE FIFTY STATES—and this book is to tell you they are there and to use your own ingenuity in seeking them out in their specific hiding places. However, if you wish some special stone and it is not close to your own hearth, the best idea is to hire a car if you don't own one, because most of the mines are off the main roads.

Never invade private property without asking permission to mine there. In the beginning, as has been stated often, it is infinitely better to surface mine where only watering the gem gravel is necessary—or where raking the ground for stones is possible Also, do it where other people are also mining and where gemstones have already been found. Even though there may be sixty or more people at some mines I know of, I also know that most of them will go home with gemstones if the area has been recently bulldozed.

Gem mining is one of the most healthful, most economical of all holidays, especially for families. The mines are seldom in a spot where you can "eat out," so the fun of a picnic lunch is mixed with the possibility of finding something that resembles the Cullinan Diamond. The main attribute of a good miner is optimism. It never occurred to me that I would not find gems in quantity. At the time I began mining that is just what I wanted—NUMBERS. Now, I know considerably more about their beauty and values and I am interested in quality as well. Knowing that a beautiful rhodolite garnet could turn up in my box at Ruth Holbrook's place in the Cowee Valley, as well as the more likely ruby or sapphire, makes the gem hunt more of a fascination than ever.

There is something else you can do on one of these mining safaris. You can take a friend for each, or perhaps just one, of the children, if they will fit in the car. That is a foolproof way for you to enjoy the experience of gem hunting, as children have eyes like eagles and discover things you will plod on to find. "The more the merrier" is truly said of a gem hunting expedition. When there were legions of us mining it was always more fun and more exciting than when the party dwindled to only four. The sharing of "finds"—the comparing of size and shade—the help each gives the other in recognizing an am-I-a-gemstone, all make the holiday more gala. Children who have friends along who are near their own age explore things about them more thoroughly.

My small nephew, Anthony Bolton, was invited by a friend to join their party panning for gold in Alaska. There were several other children in the family but the additional child was a help rather than a hindrance because he annexed one member of the family circle and left fewer to be entertained in the way children without playmates always lean on parents during a holiday. In any event, it is a good deed that will bring you many rewards and certainly the blessings of the home circle from which you have plucked one small, healthy body. There's enormous family involvement in gem mining and I have seen it in action. It is a chance for a family to be united in planning for the trip, in making the journey, and in the many things that will be done for months after the return home.

After one has had his initial mining finds polished and cut, the age-old urge to do-it-yourself will loom for most men. Oddly, women have a great interest in cutting and polishing their own gems until they discover how minute the calculations must be to protect the weight of the gems. Then, it becomes a mathematical problem and the wise thing seems to be to leave the gem cutting to who will do it perfectly and the lady will just WEAR THE GEMS.

Actually, the cost of having gems cut near the mining areas is quite reasonable. Unless prices zoom before this gets into print the price of a cabochon cut, and most of mine were cut en cabochon because of the many asteriated stones, will run between $6.50 and $8.00 a stone. Some people prefer to take their finds home and use gemologists closer to their living area but the men who are near the mining regions know the stones so thoroughly and so keenly they will give you the best advice, and the best price, very probably.

Well, what do you do for an encore once you have mined away last year's Christmas present? You have the stones set in cherishable gifts for the family. These are remembrances they will treasure—they will indeed be *family heirlooms*.

You will find you are extraordinarily creative about "his" and "hers" jewelry. You might even initiate a family ring. Instead of a family crest, choose a stone such as tourmaline— which won't turn up everywhere you look, and make it the object of your search. It will prove a wonderful memento of a "different" holiday. And it will almost certainly become your own personal family talisman.

If you are single—how about scooping up a caravan of friends and instead of two weeks at the beach why not go on a gem hunt? This could be more fun than anyone bargained for because the tastes of each person, especially adults, are so divergent. Each of you will want to track down something different in mineral life and you won't be bogged down to two weeks of seeking out one kind of gemstone. You just might find it the most economical holiday you have ever had—as well as the most exciting. There are things to be done in various parts of the country that don't surface at a glance, so explore all the possibilities for joining the natives, wherever you are, in their fun feasts, which, somehow, also become yours.

There is something else that can be interesting. Clothing today is almost as important as eating. As a matter of fact this generation of people, young and old, are, or seem to be, more interested in what they will wear than in what they will put in their mouths. You can find some of the most creative ideas you have ever encountered in the outfits worn at mining sites. If designers begin to follow the "mining mania" trail, you can be sure some interesting outfits will come out of the work-rooms across the country—and they won't be worn only by "miners."

One other facet of gem mining or gemstone hunting is important. Most of us are a bit slovenly in our intellectual habits, and lacking perception of the things around us is a major flaw in people today. "Causes" we have in abundance, criticism is the easiest kind of conversation, but counting our blessings, whether they come out of the earth or drop from the sky, is another matter. Here is an opportunity for children and parents to become involved in something that will not only immerse them in geological and mineralogical wonders, but will lead them off into all kinds of far-off what-is-its? For instance, when you know a gemstone like the alexandrite is so rare, you will want to go wherever you can find one. Jade is so old you will try to discover a piece that has the hand of time on it, and tracing the history of a jade carving is sometimes as interesting as owning the possession one is pursuing. Knowing how a ruby graduates in value, as its size increases, in a way no other gemstone does, should make anyone look for that piece of red corundum as big as a butternut.

The interest in reading and exploring that children will

have on the subject after one exposure to a mining safari is incalculable. Try it for size and know what it means to point small heads toward a most absorbing and rewarding hobby— which just might turn out to be a profession, of sorts. My own interest in mining generally grew out of an initial interest in archaeology. But I also had a grandmother who was an Egyptologist so I guess it was inevitable that the ruby safari friend would find my genes were turned toward the corundum mines from the day I opened my eyes. Years ago I went down into a "dig" in the Mound of the Hostages at Tara in Ireland. Professor O'Riordan, the famous archaeologist, and his team had just discovered relics of the Mid-Bronze Age and I was just in time to examine artifacts like pottery and bugle beads. The remains of the young prince or whoever it was they had unearthed had been removed by the time I arrived. A child who sees the interesting things that can be found in the earth due to nature's own hand will undoubtedly have an interest in things that have been buried through the intervention of man through the centuries. In any event, the road to mining has many turnings and extends a long way, so don't be too sure what you may find when you arrive. There are more surprises than just a bagful of gemstones.

32

❧

Why?

This book hasn't been written only so that you will have one more beautiful adventure, and *that* a practical one. A primal reason was to lure with the most human artifice, gem-studded gains, people with sleeping spirit to some knowledge of the glory world around them.

If you can walk in a garden and find hedgerows of fuchsia with snapping red tongues and lilacs heavy on the nearest bush and know what is their language, then you are ready to speak in the accents of gemstones, as well.

It won't happen in an hour, because like most growth, it is likely to come in stages, but one day you will look deep into the heart of a ruby or find yourself almost mesmerized by the green siren singing in a particular emerald. You will not only have discovered those gems but you will have added something to you. Rose diamonds won't be just something in the frame of an eighteenth century miniature painting; topaz won't remain only the stone on which a long-ago cameo was engraved. Some sapphire, somewhere, will have special significance for you because you brought it from the earth, watched it from its rawest form evolve into a gem of staggering beauty. If the dimension of sentimentality lies within you, there will be a need in you to see those gems you have mined set in some special frame of your choice, if not creation, to enhance, as beauty added to beauty always does, the person of the wearer.

If you find only one ruby, or if your treasure hunt unearths only a rope of miniature sapphires for your wrist, you will cherish them as keepsakes of special feeling. And—if you find a diamond—remembering the legend that encircled its brilliance from antiquity—one can only hope that all the constancy of its promise is yours.

Gems are stones of the centuries. They are a reminder of yesterday, some of the best treasure that goes back millions of years. A gemstone lasts in beauty a very long time. Bubbles burst, cities are buried in dust, iron rusts, and silks and satins crumble but the gemstone tumbles out of the earth year after year, dazzling, mysterious, soothing, and belonging to every age.

Man lives deeply with only a few of the goods that surround him. Nature is free. We must find out how to enjoy our heritage of freedom. We bind ourselves within four walls for a prescribed period of time with promises to enjoy the other side of the mountain *someday*. If "someday" isn't now, we are only half living. Nature is crammed with good things, but our only salute to it is to wait for the sun to come out long enough for two months every summer for each of us to get a sunburned midriff during beach bake-outs. Nature has twelve months of gifts for us, whether we live in the middle of a factory town or on the edge of the desert. Just remember those anthills spilling with garnets on the Navajo reservation! Gems, precious stones, jewelry—however you wish to think of them—are some of the real arrows of civilization, a most elevated form of it.

When I was doing the chapter on the feeling people have for gems I was staggered by the apathy of some of the respondents to my questions. I believe the most telling answers came from a young college girl who said: "Emeralds? I think of magnificence and palaces and something out of the ordinary. Pearls? I think of oysters and the beach and swimming. Diamonds? Weddings. Rubies? I think of museums, precious gems. But—I consider them *outside* my life. Gems are something I would *not* want to own. My friends don't have any. They are so expensive. Something of a waste. But then I don't understand original paintings either. Why would anyone buy an original painting when she can buy a copy so much cheaper?"

Maybe someday she will explore the other world, for surely there is a great, wide world outside the facsimile place she wants to live with—and in. Maybe someday when being young is over she will want to find out what went on around her that she left unexplored for so many burning moons.

"The whole point of education," said Edward Leen, the philosopher, "is human happiness." If we educate ourselves to enjoy the natural things around us as a prelude to training our powers, uncountable chapters of pleasurable reward should be in front of us. Man must elaborate his talents into results, and recognition of the things that will magnify our happiness is a talent that could have deeply satisfying results.

Happiness is not a single vertical pike. It is a wide picture that includes the photographer—and gem mining is a happy hobby that warms the world of those who "dig."